THE ANGLO-SAXONS IN 100 FACTS

MARTIN WALL

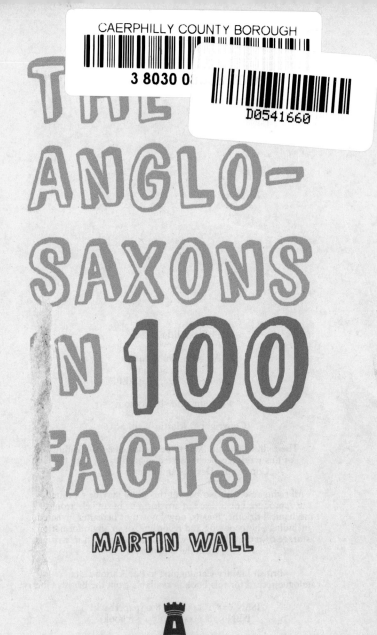

AMBERLEY

By the same author:
The Anglo-Saxon Age: The Birth of England

First published 2016

Amberley Publishing
The Hill, Stroud
Gloucestershire, GL5 4EP

www.amberley-books.com

British Library Cataloguing in Publication Data.
A catalogue record for this book is available from the British Library.

ISBN 978 1 4456 5638 0 (paperback)
ISBN 978 1 4456 5639 7 (ebook)

Typeset in 11pt on 13.5pt Sabon.
Typesetting and Origination by Amberley Publishing.
Printed in the UK.

Contents

Introduction

The Anglo-Saxons did not originate in England. They came from four Germanic tribes whose homelands lay overseas. The Saxons originally lived between the mouths of the Rivers Elbe and Weser in northern Germany. The Angles came from Angeln, in modern Schleswig-Holstein on the border between Germany and Denmark. The Jutes came from Jutland and the area approximating to modern Denmark, and the Frisians dwelt in the coastal areas around the Netherlands, though many of their ancestors were Angles and Jutes who had settled there. Into the mix there were a few Franks, Batavians, and bands of other Germanic tribal peoples. Their languages were so similar that they could easily understand each other, and their religion, culture, and their daily lives were virtually identical. But they were also proud of what made them different and fiercely defended their independent status, personified by their kings. The king of each tribe was a semi-divine being descended from gods, most importantly Woden, their chief god. Woden was the god of (among other things) war and these folk were warrior peoples, fierce, aggressive, bloodthirsty and 'dangerous to know'. Behind them other 'barbarian' peoples were on the move – Goths, Vandals, Alans, Suevi, Lombards and Burgundians and many more. These were being pushed west in their turn by the most cruel and savage horde of them all – the Huns, Asiatic nomads whose cavalry moved at lightning speed. It is therefore little wonder that the Anglo-Saxons began to look for better opportunities, and like so many before and after them they decided to emigrate ... to Britain.

1. The Anglo-Saxons Were Hired Mercenaries

The most civilised, prosperous and Romanised parts of Britain lay in the south and east, and the least developed and poorer parts in the north and west. Paradoxically the parts the Anglo-Saxons settled in were in the most Roman part of the island. The Celtic peoples of the north and west, called Britons, held out for many centuries, and even though Roman technology and learning dwindled away there rapidly, these Celts emphasised their connections to the empire for many hundreds of years. Aristocratic families ruling Celtic tribal districts or provinces had been incorporated into the Roman system of local government. When the Romans left, these high-born nobles assumed control over their own traditional lands. They formed a council to elect one of them as a 'head-man' or 'over-lord', a sort of petty dictator, known in Latin as a *Superbus Tyrannus*. In later legends and histories a person called 'Vortigern' is mentioned. This name means something like 'great clan-chief' and so it has been supposed that he was this elected leader of Britain.

Vortigern was in a fix. We don't know precisely when he came to power but it was probably in the 420s and 430s. By this time the Roman army was long gone and the Picts (from modern Scotland) and the Scots (confusingly from Ireland ... all to be explained later) were raiding in the north and west and threatening the south and east too. Vortigern, though he had a high-sounding title, actually had no real power, no effective armed forces to defend Britain. It seems that Vortigern decided to get himself a bit of muscle. He invited Jutish and Saxon war-bands to come to Britain to act as a mercenary army (and navy) with the objective, or so he said, of kicking out the Picts. The

Saxon war-bands traditionally landed at Ebbsfleet in Kent. Tradition states that Vortigern granted more and more land to the Saxons, and married the daughter of the pagan chieftain, Hengist, putting away his former wife, by whom he had three sons. These sons rebelled against him, and this was the signal for Ambrosius, a powerful magnate, to defy Vortigern. Eventually at a conference between the Saxons and the British the Saxons produced concealed knives and slaughtered the British tribal leaders, taking Vortigern prisoner. Large areas of the south-east were ceded to the Saxons. By now the Saxon colony was overcrowded and more and more of their compatriots were arriving. Vortigern was discredited and powerless, and Ambrosius was raising a British army against them.

2. The First Anglo-Saxons in England Were Neither Angles nor Saxons

According to the *Anglo-Saxon Chronicle*, the people Vortigern had hired were not Angles or Saxons but Jutes, or at least they were led by two 'brothers' who were Jutes – Hengist and Horsa. They may actually have been brothers, but Anglo-Saxon warriors thought of their shipmates and comrades-in-arms fraternally, a bit like modern-day gangsters. These notions of close-knit military honour were elevated by them to the status of sacred traditions. To make a deal on trust was, in their eyes, to enter into an irrevocable bargain to honour and respect the man with whom one had done business. To walk away from the deal was to insult the man, and all his kinsfolk. This called for blood-vengeance and war usually commenced immediately.

The Anglo-Saxons and others broke out and burned southern Britain from coast to coast, sacking towns and slaughtering anyone they could find. Nowhere in these areas was safe, and there was nothing to stop them, but in the north and west there were at least some Britons with troops of their own. To escape the anarchy and bloodshed many Britons fled overseas to Armorica in Gaul, still called 'Brittany' to this day. Others fled west, into Devon and Cornwall, the West Midlands, and what is now Wales. Many Britons could not flee, however, and those that survived in the south and east now found they had new overlords, the Angles, Saxons ... and Jutes!

3. The Anglo-Saxons Were Halted By a Mysterious British Hero

Gildas, a British monk who wrote a fascinating history of these times, tells us that eventually the Romano-Britons rallied and organised resistance to the Anglo-Saxons, defeating them in several battles that culminated in a 'siege' at a place he called *Mons Badonicus* or 'Mount Badon'. Unfortunately he does not name any of the combatants and only tells us that the Britons won, but a later Welsh scribe called Nennius says that the leader was 'Arthur' and that he slew 960 Saxons. Nennius was writing hundreds of years later, when Wales had become a separate country and culture with its own legendary traditions of this 'King Arthur'. He may have used material which contained poetic references to a mythical folk-hero, and then interpolated them into his history. The truth about Arthur is that we just don't know if he existed as a real-life leader or not. But somebody did indeed defeat the Saxons in this mysterious battle. The most likely candidate was Ambrosius Aurelianus, who certainly did exist in Amesbury in Wiltshire and other places in southern England are named after him. He was a high-born noble and the main enemy of Vortigern. He may have led a faction dedicated to maintaining Roman traditions and civilisation and Roman Catholic religion. He had an august Roman name and may have known something about Roman military tactics, but he must have been very wealthy and powerful to train and equip an army from scratch. Some people think that 'Artorius' or Arthur may have been a nephew to him, but as I say, this is only speculation.

The Anglo-Saxons were still in control of their own areas, however, and even though some of them decided to abandon Britain, many more remained. For about fifty years there was an uneasy truce, but whoever the British leader who had halted the Anglo-Saxons was, as soon as he was dead the British part of the island disintegrated into a patchwork of small tribal kingdoms. Gildas is our most reliable historical source for this period, and he says he was born in the year of the victory at Mount Badon. Unfortunately he was not a historian in the sense we think of that term, but had his own agenda. He used his book to calumniate and berate the Celtic leaders of his time, especially for their lack of Christian morality. Why didn't he mention this 'Arthur'? It was as if someone writing a history of Britain at the end of the twentieth century had neglected to mention Winston Churchill! There are many theories about this, one being that Gildas *did* record him in a sort of acrostic code, and that when we de-code these references 'Arthur' is revealed to be Cuneglas, a British chieftain whom he calls 'the bear' (Arthur means 'bear'). Cuneglas is one of the 'five tyrants' of Britain upon whom he heaps so much opprobrium. It is unlikely that we will ever really know the truth of the matter.

4. THE FIRST SAXON KING HAD A BRITISH NAME

It is strange that one of the first Saxon kings had a British name, Cerdic. Our present monarch, Elizabeth II, is supposed to be a distant descendant of him. Cerdic was supposed to have been the first King of Wessex, one of the seven kingdoms the Anglo-Saxons established in what had formerly been Britain. Now that literacy was a thing of the past, it was very difficult to construct complicated histories, but it was vitally important for the Anglo-Saxon kings to be able to prove their right to rule by virtue of being descended from important men or gods. They achieved this by encouraging a class of men with the capacity for prodigious feats of memory, called *scops, skalds* or bards. These men committed the history of the tribe and the genealogy of its kings to memory, and recounted their deeds around the cooking fires in the royal halls. Over time these memories were garbled and perhaps deliberately altered. Only after hundreds of years had elapsed were any of them written down. There is something odd about Cerdic. He was supposed to have been King of the West Saxons, but the area which he was supposed to have ruled has yielded virtually nothing in the way of Saxon archaeology. Even before the Anglo-Saxons had arrived in Britain, the Romans had settled bands of Germanic soldiers in Britain to guard against attack. One of these tribes, the *Gewissae*, had been living in the Thames Valley area for a long time, so long in fact that they had probably intermarried with British womenfolk. Once the Romans had left they were in a good position to assert themselves as overlords in the area, and it could be that in intertribal conflicts they prevailed. It would not be unusual for one of their kings to have had a British name. We will probably never know, because much of the history of what we call 'the Dark Ages' is speculative, obscure and throws up more questions than answers. Whoever Cerdic was, the kingdom he was said to have founded, Wessex, rapidly expanded and was soon in a position to compete for control of all southern Britain.

5. 'England' Was Comprised Of Seven Anglo-Saxon Kingdoms

There were seven major Anglo-Saxon kingdoms, each with their own ruling dynasties, called the 'Heptarchy' (meaning 'seven'). We have already looked at Wessex in the south, but 'next door' was the small kingdom of Sussex. Along the south coast lay Kent, probably the oldest of them all. Then came Essex, the kingdom of the East Saxons, and to the north of them was East Anglia. In the Midlands there was a kingdom of the Middle-Angles, which eventually morphed into the mighty kingdom of Mercia, which became the most powerful of them all for a time. In the north two Anglian kingdoms, Bernicia and Deira, merged to become the great nation of Northumbria. As well as these nations there were numerous British nations and mini-states in the north and west, all of whom were the traditional enemies of the Anglo-Saxons and engaged in constant warfare with them.

These complex territorial configurations were in a constant state of flux. Because the Anglo-Saxons had a common enemy in the British we may think that they should have 'stuck together' and cooperated with each other. Actually, they did exactly the opposite. Their loyalties were strictly tribal and based on strong bonds with their kin and traditional oaths to their kings. Each Anglo-Saxon kingdom saw itself as pre-eminent in some way, and none of them was prepared to give up its independence, at least at first. However, the largest and most populous were bound to prevail in the end, and eventually the four most powerful Anglo-Saxon nations eclipsed their smaller rivals, Wessex, East Anglia, Northumbria and Mercia. Each of these four aimed to become the dominant Anglo-Saxon power in the centuries that followed, but which of them would succeed?

6. Slavery Was Commonplace in Anglo-Saxon Times

All the Germanic tribes kept slaves. The name they gave to the peoples who lived in the great forests and mountains to the east of Germany, 'Slavs', gives us a clue about their relationship with them. Slav means 'slave'. The Germanic tribes who came to Britain were no different. They thought that anyone who did not share their language and culture as inferior and when they first encountered a Celtic tribe in Europe called the *Volcae* they thought the name extended to everyone speaking Celtic languages, not just this local tribe. Over time this name became *Weallas*, meaning 'strangers' or 'foreigners', and individual Celts were called *Walh*. When they encountered Celtic people in Britain they gave this name to them, the 'Welsh', and the country where they predominated became 'Wales', the 'land of the foreigners'. This may seem to us a rather contemptuous way to treat one's neighbours but the Anglo-Saxons knew nothing about multiculturalism or the tolerance of difference, and we would be foolish to try to impose our own modern notions of 'political correctness' onto them. Their social ideas were simple and, in their way, honest. Either you were in the tribe, working hard for its lords and kings, doing your duty in times of war, performing your devotions on the pagan holy days, and speaking the language of the Germanic forefathers, or you were not.

There is a long-standing notion that the word *Weallas* had another connotation, meaning 'slaves'. This is disputed, but there may be something in it. By the sixth century, the Anglo-Saxon population was increasing rapidly, whereas the British population had been decimated by plague and mass emigration.

Despite this, those of British descent must still have outnumbered the Anglo-Saxon incomers and many, if not most, probably lived in the areas they controlled. Most likely these British were not slaves as we imagine them but a class called 'bond-labourers' who were allowed to stay on, but had more limited rights than a free man. Undoubtedly there would have been slaves who had been taken as prisoners of war, both British and from other Anglo-Saxon nations. Criminals could be punished by being forced into slavery too. We live in an age when slavery is despised as a cruel and immoral practice, and rightly so, but this was not the case back then. The Roman Empire was founded on slavery, and the Anglo-Saxon social order was no different. Indeed, the British Empire was predicated upon slavery in more recent times!

7. J. R. R. TOLKIEN BASED *THE LORD OF THE RINGS* ON ANGLO-SAXON MERCIA

Many millions of people all over the world have read *The Hobbit* or *The Lord of the Rings* trilogy, or have watched the cinematic productions of these works, but perhaps not many realise that they were not merely products of J. R. R. Tolkien's vivid imagination. Tolkien was born in South Africa but returned to England with his mother and younger brother at the age of three. Unfortunately when his father died in South Africa the family were left in in quite impoverished circumstances. The family lived in Birmingham, a large industrial city in the Midlands; not the sort of place, we might think, which would evoke strong connections with Anglo-Saxon times, but for the young Tolkien this was the very heart of the Anglo-Saxon world. Tolkien grew up at the edge of the city, on the border with Worcestershire. His mother converted to Roman Catholicism and, with help from a friendly priest, he and his brother were tutored and gained an excellent education. The harsh discipline and devotion he gained from his studies was supplemented by an extraordinary capacity to see a rich 'otherworld' inherent in the beautiful English countryside on his doorstep; the uplands and woods of the Clent and Lickey Hills, the distant peaks of Malvern, even Moseley Bog and Sarehole Mill just round the corner from his humble home, became transfigured into magical landscapes.

What the small boy had realised was that, once upon a time, Birmingham had been part of one of the most powerful Anglo-Saxon nations, Mercia. Eventually he became a professor of Anglo-Saxon and Scandinavian Literature at Oxford, but he never forgot his Mercian roots. The strange magical otherworld of the Anglo-Saxons obsessed him, a world populated by light-elves, dragons and wizards, a realm suffused with elemental energies. Mercia was one of the kingdoms which retained its Anglo-Saxon culture and dialects longest – indeed, it still does! In the landscape just beyond the edge of the city he explored places which were still uncontaminated by modernity. Some people think he may have based Hobbiton, the underground dwelling places of the Hobbits, on the Kinver Rock Houses near to Stourbridge. A few miles away from Kinver there is a tiny hamlet called Drakelow with similar cave dwellings, and a landscape which so resembles Hobbiton as to be uncanny.

8. Out of the Forest a Tribe of Witches Emerged

We have already looked at the obscure and mysterious tribe called the *Gewissae* who may have had something to do with the emergence of Wessex. No one really knows the 'facts' because they are shrouded in mystery, but a tribe with a similar name, the *Hwicce* (pronounced 'witch-a') moved into the region of Gloucestershire and Worcestershire during the late sixth century. Britain was very much more forested in those days than it is today, especially in the western realms, and the social dislocation caused by the constant warfare encouraged the process for a while. In Oxfordshire there was a forest called Wychwood which still exists in a diminished form today. 'Wyche' is a form of *Hwicce*.

It used to be thought that there was a stark divide between the Christian British and the heathen Anglo-Saxons, but a fascinating theory has been promulgated recently by an archaeologist, Stephen J. Yeates. Although his theory is speculative it cannot be lightly dismissed. He believes that the *Dobunni* had preserved a priestly class who venerated a pre-Christian deity called *Cuda*, a nature goddess of rivers and hill-top groves called *Nemetons* and that the Cotswolds are named after her. He adduces archaeological and place-name evidence to support the idea that when the *Hwicce* supplanted the previous culture they continued the cult well into the early medieval period. In his view the subsequent name of the tribe is no accident, and he thinks it means that they were literally 'the tribe of witches'.

9. THE BRITONS WERE PUSHED FURTHER WEST

The strategic situation in Britain had changed radically by the end of the sixth century. The three powerful Anglo-Saxon kingdoms on the Britons' frontiers, Wessex in the south, Mercia in the Midlands, and Northumbria in the north, all began to push west. In the south, a powerful king called Ceawlin overran Wiltshire, Dorset, parts of Devon and Somerset and the area around the lower Severn. In the north, a new king of a consolidated Northumbria, Aethelric, struck over the Pennines into Rheged, a large Celtic territory between Galloway and Lancashire. The *Gwr y Gogledd*, or 'men of the north' as these northern Celts were called, were no pushover. Their mighty king, Urien, defeated the Northumbrians and concluded alliances with the fierce Celtic tribes on the Scottish borders. He hit back and drove the Northumbrians onto the island now called Lindisfarne, and almost into the sea. But at the moment of triumph he was assassinated by a jealous Celtic rival. The Celtic alliance fell apart and the Northumbrians rallied around a new king, Aethelfrith. In turn he attacked Owain, Urien's son, and after an epic struggle Rheged fell as well. This terrible war, which had so nearly ended in disaster, turned Northumbria into a fearsome war-machine. Aethelfrith attempted to overthrow the kings of Powys and Gwynedd in north Wales and in an epic battle at Chester the Welsh king was killed. Many hundreds of British monks who had gone to pray for a British victory were cruelly slaughtered by Aethelfrith, who thought their prayers might be a form of magic worked against him.

It was not just in the south and the north that the Anglo-Saxons were on the move. A king called Creoda set himself up as king of a new entity, Mercia, in the Midlands. Mercia means 'border country', as in the Welsh 'Marches'. The border indicated was the frontier with the British tribes of the Midlands. At first the Anglian invaders were confined to the East Midlands. Nottingham was founded by an Anglo-Saxon leader called Snot, and was originally 'Snottingham'! Gradually, following the course of the River Trent, the Mercians arrived at the watershed between the Trent and the Severn, on the high ground of Staffordshire and Warwickshire, roughly where the West Midlands conurbation is today. Here they established a royal capital at Tamworth. Although we know very little about them, because they were among the last Anglo-Saxons to convert to Christianity (and so to have a literate culture), it seems certain that by the end of the sixth century they had penetrated as far as the belt of forests and marshes called Morfe and Kinver, and had probably imposed tribute arrangements on the remaining British kingdoms in the West Midlands. These doughty pioneers were soon to unite under a powerful king, and to become the mightiest of the Anglo-Saxon realms.

10. In Britain's Darkest Hour, an Anglo-Saxon Poem Came Vividly to Life

Just one week before the outbreak of the Second World War in 1939, archaeologists made a stunning discovery at Sutton Hoo in East Anglia. It was a burial mound containing an Anglo-Saxon ship, and within the ship a mighty king had been laid to rest surrounded by his treasures, just as the mythical hero Beowulf had been in the oldest English epic poem of the same name. The artefacts were of a breath-taking quality and beauty, the greatest treasure ever found in England at the time, perhaps at any time. The most famous of them was a helmet, decorated with exquisitely worked foils and a menacing face-guard which has become *the* image of the Anglo-Saxon era. There were other weapons: a superb sword with gold and garnet fittings, a shield decorated with a dragon and stylised bird, a battleaxe and spears. These were all weapons of a mighty warrior, and there was even a whetstone to keep them sharpened. Silver bowls and drinking horns for the feasting in the home of the gods were provided, and a lyre so that the king should be entertained there. Silver spoons, bronze bowls and the king's personal jewellery were interred too, including a gold buckle weighing one pound with interlaced designs of such intricacy and delicate workmanship that it is hard to imagine them being reproduced by any craftsman alive today. Forty coins were also provided to pay the oarsmen of the ship as they sailed into the afterlife. The actual body of the king was missing or had disintegrated, but the obvious question remained – who was this man?

The action of *Beowulf* takes place in Sweden and Denmark, but it was composed in England. The East Anglian royal house, called *Wuffingas*, may have been descended from a Swedish royal dynasty called the *Scylfings*. The helmet is very similar to ones which have been discovered in Sweden and it may have been made there before the Anglo-Saxon emigration had even commenced, a treasured heirloom hallowed by many generations of use. If it is the case that the East Anglian kings had these strong connections with Sweden, then it could be that *Beowulf* was actually composed as a tribute to these important connections, implying that the king buried at Sutton Hoo had been Beowulf incarnate. Many people think that the man buried at Sutton Hoo was King Raedwald of East Anglia. A little later on we will hear more about him.

11. A Chance Meeting in Rome Initiated the Anglo-Saxon Conversion to Christianity

One day a young clergyman called Gregory happened to be walking through the slave market in Rome when he noticed a small group of children for sale. They had pale skin, blonde hair and striking blue eyes and Gregory asked the dealer where these youngsters came from. The answer he received intrigued him. They were Angles from Deira, part of Northumbria, and Gregory could not help making a punning reply that they looked more like 'Angels' from God. The smiling slave trader shocked Gregory by telling him that, far from being angels, these were the children of fearsome heathen barbarians who knew nothing of the Christian God. After many years Gregory became Pope Gregory the Great, and it now lay within his power to send a mission to the Anglo-Saxons and bring them the good news.

It was a job no-one wanted. The Anglo-Saxons had a bad reputation. The man Gregory chose for the mission, Augustine, was arrogant, small-minded, and vacillating. He tried desperately to be released from the task but Gregory was determined and in 597 Augustine's party of missionaries were allowed to land at Thanet in Kent. They came ashore with great trepidation, singing the litany and bearing before them a cross of silver and an image of Christ painted on a board. The menacing stares of the Kentish soldiers must have intimidated them but the man they were going to meet was just as fearful of them. King Aethelberht of Kent already knew something about Christianity; he was married to a Christian princess from France, and he had allowed her and her chaplain to celebrate mass and to refurbish a ruined old Roman church. Aethelberht wanted to encourage trade with France and to imitate some of their innovations but he had to tread carefully. His noblemen and subjects were fiercely loyal to the old gods, like Woden, and there was a suspicion that this new religion was a form of magic or enchantment. Therefore, the king would not meet Augustine indoors, but chose to meet him outside beneath the shade of a protective oak tree. This mutual mistrust soon dissipated and Augustine was allowed to proselytise and baptise many of the king's subjects. Gregory sent instructions to extend the hierarchical Church structure to other parts of the country too, but Augustine soon found he had big problems. Pope Gregory's ideas about the Anglo-Saxon lands were naive and out of date. Aethelberht's protection did not extend far outside his own kingdom of Kent, and so despite London being Gregory's favoured centre for an archbishopric, Augustine had to be content with Canterbury, where it has remained to this day. As well as this, Augustine was not the only game in town. The British had their own Church and the Irish missionary Columba had initiated a mission in the far north. He had died in the same year Augustine landed. So despite what most of us learned in school, Augustine did not land in a completely pagan island, and he had a big job ahead of him.

12. A Hunted Exile Became the Most Powerful Anglo-Saxon King

Aethelfrith forced a claimant to the throne of Deira, Edwin, into exile. Edwin fled to the court of Cadfan ap Iago at Aberffraw in Gwynedd. A royal exile could claim the protection of the king, usually in exchange for promises of future good relations should his fortunes change, and of course any intelligence he could supply about mutual enemies. Selyf of Powys and Edwin had such a mutual enemy, Aethelfrith, but when Selyf was killed at the battle of Chester Edwin had to flee again, this time to the court of King Ceorl of Mercia. Ceorl did not want a war with Aethelfrith, even though he supported Edwin, so he compromised. After marrying off his daughter to Edwin, he encouraged him to flee yet again, this time to King Raedwald in East Anglia (remember him?) and by this time Edwin had become a very 'hot potato'.

King Raedwald was a *Bretwalda* (overlord), acknowledged as pre-eminent among the Anglo-Saxon kings. Edwin had run out of options and Aethelfrith would not rest content until Edwin was dead; he even sent a request to Raedwald to murder Edwin, but he was saved from this fate by the intervention of Raedwald's wife, who pleaded for him. Raedwald decided to risk everything and march on Northumbria. In a terrible battle on the River Idle in Lindsey, Raedwald's son was killed by Aethelfrith who had mistaken him for Edwin (there is a tradition that they had swapped armour, to bring them luck in battle). The furious Raedwald stormed Aethelfrith's position and killed him in turn and the Northumbrians were routed, the river turning red with their blood. Raedwald, still in mourning for his son, effectively installed

Edwin as the new King of Northumbria in 616. After exiling Aethelfrith's sons, Oswald and Oswy, Edwin had been crowned as king and determined to extend Northumbrian power. He attacked a small weak Celtic kingdom called Elmet which was easily overwhelmed, but the annexation of this tiny country sparked a wider conflict. The Mercians were unhappy with Edwin's adventures on their frontiers but wanted to avoid war. A more belligerent adversary was Gwynedd whose king, Cadwallon ap Cadfan, greatly feared Edwin's fleet in western waters.

Edwin was ambitious and ruthless. His wife and queen was a Roman Catholic from Kent. Paulinus, her personal chaplain, was determined to convert the king to Roman ways. York, Edwin's capital, was the second largest city in Anglo-Saxon England. The magnificent ruins of the Roman city were still standing, and it may be that Edwin came to see himself as the heir to the 'Dux Britanniarum', the old Roman title of the governor of the north. Edwin took to processing through his capital with a Roman-style *tufa* (standard) borne before him as a symbol of his authority. In 627 Edwin was baptised and many thousands of his subjects followed. Bishop Paulinus performed mass-baptism ceremonies in the River Glen near Yeavering, one of Edwin's huge royal palaces. A huge timber stadium was erected there, from which Paulinus proselytised the people. Tens of thousands were converted and Edwin had the full backing of the Roman Church, making Northumbria into a sort of Anglo-Saxon super-state.

13. Horses Were Sacred Animals

The English have always been known for their love of horses but this may well derive from their ancient reverence for these animals as intermediaries to the gods. The two brothers who had initiated the Anglo-Saxon invasion, Hengist and Horsa, both had a name which meant 'horse'. They landed under a banner of a white horse, still the emblem of the county of Kent to this day. White horses were especially sacred. These were taken by the high priests and corralled in paddocks hedged round with nut-bearing trees. The priests had a taboo on riding horses, and when Northumbria converted to Christianity the high priest, Coifi, demonstrated his apostasy by mounting a horse and riding out to demolish the pagan shrines and spear the idols through as a sign of his disenchantment with the old religion. Woden himself had gained his sacred knowledge by transforming the tree he had climbed, *Yggdrasil,* into an eight-legged horse called *Sleipnir* ('the slippery one'). On holy days these sacred horses were yoked to a cart and followed on by the king and his chief priest. Their neighing and their stepping over spears were supposed to indicate good and evil fortunes in store for the tribe, especially in war. Only a king could ride one of these creatures or, perhaps, a powerful wizard such as Gandalf in *The Lord of the Rings.*

There seem to have been some exceptions. There are depictions of Pictish soldiers being ridden down by Bernician mounted troops and this shows that the Anglo-Saxons were quite capable, had they so wished, of using cavalry. At the battle of Stamford Bridge in 1066 it is recorded that the English army used light cavalry and archers, but this was right at the end of

The Anglo-Saxons in 100 Facts

28

the Anglo-Saxon period when they had been influenced by other foreign innovations and had forgotten their pagan heritage. In general, it was 'not cricket' to fight on horseback, or to use a bow and arrow, and the Anglo-Saxons fought in the main as infantry and expected their opponents to do the same. This was to contribute to their eventual undoing, as we will see later on.

14. A Petty Snub Elicited a Fateful Prophecy

Augustine's mission had precariously survived in its small enclave around Canterbury. We should have some sympathy with the poor man, who was isolated from the rest of the civilised world amid people whose way of life must have seemed to him primitive and harsh. As if that wasn't enough, he was under constant pressure from his remote boss, the Pope. Gregory still thought Britain was full of grand cities and roads in good order and failed to understand just how much Britain had deteriorated since the Roman departure. He was prepared to compromise on some things, however. Augustine was exhorted to implant Christian churches on the site of former heathen shrines so that the people would accept them more readily, but for all this Augustine and his few followers had been given a seemingly impossible task. Therefore he decided to summon the bishops of the Britons to a meeting on the borders between the Anglo-Saxons and the Celts, possibly at Aust in Gloucestershire or Great Witley in Worcestershire.

The Britons were suspicious of Augustine's motives, so before they went to meet him they visited a Celtic holy man, to seek his advice. The hermit told them that if when they approached him Augustine rose from his episcopal chair to greet them then this would be a sign of his good faith, and that they should co-operate with him, but if Augustine remained seated then this indicated that he was a haughty man with whom they should transact no business. When it came down to it Augustine remained seated because as far as he was concerned he was an envoy of the Pope, whereas these British bishops represented a schismatic Church whose teaching was riddled with error. This was a bad start to the negotiations and things did not get any better. Augustine demanded that the British conform to the Roman Church in the matter of the computations for setting the date of Easter (they celebrated this on a different date) and on other more minor details. The real bombshell came when he proposed a joint effort to convert the Anglo-Saxons. The 'Saxons' (they called all Germanic peoples Saxons) were their national enemy and seemed to them scarcely human, more like devils incarnate. Augustine's tiny mission was far away and had no influence so they naturally refused. Augustine was furious and, 'in a threatening manner', he promised that if the British would not have peace with the 'brethren' then they should have war from the Anglo-Saxons, and that they would suffer 'the vengeance of death at their hands'. Needless to say, the seven British bishops and their entourage departed immediately amid considerable acrimony. Not a good start to the ecumenical project!

15. Three Mighty Kings Fought an Epic War

Augustine's mission began to fail immediately after he died. Although the new Archbishop of Canterbury remained when the people of Kent became apostate, two other bishops fled overseas. Fortunately for Rome, their fortunes were improving in Northumbria. Edwin's queen was a Christian Kentish princess and she brought with her a chaplain, Paulinus, and between them they set about converting the king. Edwin's mind was on his empire-building so he prevaricated for a long time, but did not object to Christianity being preached. In 629 Edwin's fleet attacked the Isle of Man and Anglesey (or Ynys Mon). The King of Gwynedd, Cadwallon, was taken by surprise at Penmon and forced to flee to a tiny island off the coast, now called Priestholm or 'Puffin Island'. From there he was taken off to exile in Ireland and now Edwin's bid to become master of the whole of Great Britain was becoming a reality.

The Anglo-Saxon kingdom with most to lose from Edwin's ambitions was Wessex. Their king, Cwichelm, arranged for an assassination attempt on Edwin with a poisoned dagger, but it failed, although Edwin was grievously wounded. As he fought for his life he promised that if he should recover and have victory over the West Saxons he would become a baptised Christian. Gradually he recovered and he kept his oath. Tens of thousands of his subjects were baptised in mass ceremonies. Wessex was duly punished, and in doing so Edwin had been forced to march through Mercia. Two brothers, Eowa and Penda, ruled the two halves of Mercia, the north and the south. Penda ruled in the south and so was the enemy of the West Saxons. It seemed like a good solution to Edwin to let Penda do his fighting for him and this fearsome warrior fought several campaigns against Wessex.

There now occurred one of those events upon which the fate of nations turn. Cadwallon was still at large, and he was no ordinary petty king of a small country like Elmet. His family were descendants of a king called Cunedda whose tribe, the *Votadini*, had been given land in North Wales in the early post-Roman period to defend the area against coastal raiding from the Irish. Remember what I said about the Scots being from Ireland? In fact the *Scotti* may initially have been an even bigger menace to the western coasts than the Anglo-Saxons were in the east. Cadwallon raised an army of Irish and Breton mercenaries and landed in Devon. Penda was at Exeter besieging the city and suddenly found himself threatened by this new army. Despite his daring reputation Penda had his back to the wall, but Cadwallon did not want war with him. He wanted to liberate his homeland of Gwynedd and to kill Edwin. Cadwallon offered Penda a deal. If he would join with him to destroy Edwin, Penda would have a free hand to loot Northumbria and plunder its new churches and monasteries. So now three kings had embarked on a life and death struggle for supremacy – Edwin, who had become the de facto *Bretwalda* or 'wide-ruler'; Cadwallon, whose pretensions to being 'high king' of Britain were informed by powerful bardic prophecies; and finally Penda, the ruler of the emerging state of Mercia.

16. THE SACK OF NORTHUMBRIA ENDED HOPES OF A BRITISH REVIVAL

The two allies, Cadwallon and Penda, joined forces to liberate Gwynedd. Their armies invaded from the borders of Mercia and reached Cefn Digoll, Long Mountain, near Welshpool. Here the Northumbrian army lay in wait for them but they were routed and driven out of North Wales. Cadwallon, together with Penda's Mercians, marched on Northumbria. Edwin's army confronted them at a place called *Haethfelth* which could be Hatfield Chase near Doncaster, or possibly Cuckney in Nottinghamshire. Edwin was killed together with his son Osfrith. Another son, Eadfrith, escaped only to be ruthlessly hunted down by Penda and killed later. The Welsh and Mercians pillaged Northumbria throughout the winter but Penda returned to Mercia when he had his share of loot. Cadwallon was a man with a grudge and the Welsh showed no mercy to the Northumbrian population. Northumbria was so devastated by this attack that it ceased to exist completely, breaking down into its former component parts.

It must have seemed like a hopeless situation for the Northumbrians but within months everything changed. Aethelfrith's sons, Oswald and Oswy, had been in exile on the tiny island of Iona. Schooled by Irish monks in the traditions of their founder St Columba, they had become devout Christians. Oswald raised an army in Lothian and marched into Northumbria. Cadwallon rode out to meet him just outside Hexham near Hadrian's Wall. Oswald claimed that St Columba had appeared to him in a vision promising him victory, and he drew up his army beneath a huge wooden cross. The battle which followed, called Heavenfield, in 634 was one of the most important in British history. If Cadwallon had won all of northern England would have become, in effect, part of Wales! Of course, this is not what happened: despite having a larger army Cadwallon was beaten and his army destroyed. He was trapped at a place called Denis Brook, now called Rowley Burn, and killed, ending any hopes of a British revival against the Anglo-Saxon nations.

17. King Oswald of Northumbria Met a Grim End

Oswald was preoccupied for eight years in rebuilding his stricken country. Aedan, a young monk, criss-crossed the country on foot distributing alms and comforting the people; eventually he established a monastery on the island of Lindisfarne which Oswald had given to him as a base. Initially another, more austere monk had been sent from Iona, the tiny island where Oswald and his brother Oswy had lived in exile, but he had been defeated by the 'indomitable barbarism' of the Northumbrian people. When Aedan had heard the older man's embittered account of the failure of this mission, he had remarked that maybe what was needed was 'the milk of milder doctrine', so the precocious youth had been sent as a missionary there in his stead. Aedan spoke no English and Oswald had acted as an interpreter for him when he arrived. This Irish-influenced mission became one of the glories of the Christian world and turned Northumbria into an intellectual and artistic powerhouse. Bede, the Northumbrian monk, lionised Oswald in his history of the English Church, written nearly a century later, and by then Oswald had become a saint. It was only natural that Bede should glorify this humble, pious king, who was his own countryman and a national hero, and that he should demonise Penda, the 'bad' pagan King of Mercia, Northumbria's enemy. The conflict with Penda could not be delayed, however, and in 641 Oswald invaded Mercia.

On 5 August Penda and his Welsh allies pitched battle against Oswald at a place called *Maserfelth* in English or *Maes Cogwy* in Welsh. There is a theory that the place became the town of Oswestry in

Shropshire, 'Oswald's Tree'. Penda soon overwhelmed Oswald's army. When he could see that all was lost Oswald knelt to pray for his doomed soldiers before being killed and hacked into pieces. His severed head and limbs were affixed to poles and hung on a tree as an offering to Woden, 'the grim one'. Bede interpreted this as a deliberate mockery of Oswald's religion, and there may be some truth in this. Even Penda's Welsh allies were shocked by the act. Oswy recovered Oswald's remains and had these transferred to Bardney Abbey in Lindsey.

Penda invaded Northumbria and looted it again in 644, amassing vast treasure. Wessex was invaded too, and when its king, Cenwalh, fled to East Anglia after repudiating his marriage to Penda's sister, Penda invaded East Anglia twice, killing its ruler, King Ecgric, in battle. His successor, Anna, fled into exile, but when he returned he was killed by Penda alongside his son Jurmin at the Battle of Bulcamp. East Anglia became, in effect, a client-state of Mercia. Penda had become a legendary pagan warlord in the manner of Beowulf – a man to be feared and respected – but by 655 he was probably well into his fifties, an old man for those times.

18. The Staffordshire Hoard May Be Part of Penda's Treasure

On 5 July 2009 a metal-detector enthusiast called Terry Herbert was detecting in a south Staffordshire field next to the A5, or Watling Street. The discovery he made was mind-blowing. The Staffordshire Hoard, as it is now known, is the largest hoard of Anglo-Saxon gold and jewels ever found, eleven pounds-weight in gold and over three pounds-weight in silver, but it is not the sheer amount of precious metals which is staggering, but the exquisite workmanship, inlaid with thousands of glittering blood-red garnets, in animal designs with fine filigree and cloisonné work. There are more than 4,000 individual artefacts, but they are small and it could have all fitted into a large holdall.

It is such a large find and so incredibly complex that conservation is only nearing completion and the research project is still ongoing (meaning this fact may actually turn out to be wrong!) but the general consensus is that it is thought to comprise elements of the booty looted by Penda's armies from all over the rest of England. It is made up for the most part of pommel and hilt decorations of swords, examples which would have belonged to an elite in the Anglo-Saxon warrior aristocracy, thus the exquisite jewels and precious metals, but why the obscure location? My own theory is that the nearby road is the clue. Watling Street was an old Roman road which was still in use in the 650s and beyond into our own times. A small but important town called Wall is only two miles away and ancient Welsh poetry records a battle fought there at this time. As for Penda, I think the depositing of the hoard may have something to do with the events which happened just after his death, but this is just one of many theories. The fact is that we just don't know all the answers about the Staffordshire Hoard – at least not yet!

19. THE 'SON OF DANGER' WAS BETRAYED BY HIS ALLIES

We left Penda as he was about to commence his final expedition of 655. At first events went according to plan; they could hardly do otherwise, Penda's host was immense. Oswy, the new King of Northumbria, could do nothing but retire as Penda's marauders ranged at will all over his realm. Eventually another vast tribute of treasure was given to Penda, along with Oswy's son, Ecgfrith, as a hostage. As winter came, Penda decided to withdraw and on 15 November 655, somewhere near Leeds, his progress was blocked by a swollen river called *Winwaed* which gave Oswy time to catch up with him. Oswy promised to build a dozen monasteries and give up his daughter to a nunnery if he should have the victory, but when it came down to it no divine intervention was necessary. Penda's coalition of allies was falling apart. The Welsh contingent, under their king, Cadfael *Cadomedd* 'the battle-shirker', deserted, as did the Deiran contingent. Only the East Anglians remained loyal to Penda and in the lashing rain the battle began. Eventually the Northumbrians broke through to the elderly Penda who hewed around him to the last, until he was overpowered and decapitated. He had led a life every bit as exciting and glorious as the heroes portrayed in the Anglo-Saxon sagas. The Welsh remember him as 'Panta ap Pyd', or the 'son of danger', in their poetry and he represents the last flicker of the Anglo-Saxon heroic tradition.

The war that had raged for more than two decades had a victor, Oswy of Northumbria, but the consequences for Mercia were calamitous. Peada, Penda's son, was

Oswy's son-in-law, so he installed him as a puppet king of the Middle Angles. Eventually, over Easter 656 Peada was poisoned by agents working for his wife, and for Mercia the future looked very bleak.

20. Penda's Sons Became Powerful Christian Kings

One of Penda's sons, Wulfhere, had gone into hiding until some change in fortune presented itself. Whilst Oswy was campaigning in the far north against the Picts, Wulfhere emerged from hiding and was proclaimed as the new Mercian king. The Northumbrian governors were killed or driven out and Wulfhere raised a powerful army. Oswy was forced to accept this loss of overlordship over Mercia but Wulfhere had learned the lessons of his father's eventual defeat and his brother's ill-fated conversion to Christianity. He chose a man he trusted, Trumhere, to be his new Mercian bishop. He did not renew the war with Northumbria which had cost his country so dearly. His ambition was to dominate England south of the Humber, and by intelligent relations with the Church, and subtle use of his military muscle, he gradually extended Mercian influence until he had subdued Wessex, Kent and Sussex. In the west he established the Welsh border roughly where it remains today, at a place still called 'Wulfhere's Ford' on the Severn. In the east he established the monastery of *Medeshamstede* which eventually grew into Peterborough Abbey, one of the richest monasteries in England.

Northumbria and Wessex both attempted to break Wulfhere's power towards the end of his reign, perhaps with some success, because he suddenly died of illness in 675. He was succeeded by his younger brother Aethelred, who triumphed over the Northumbrians in a huge battle on the River Trent in 679 and punished Kent for its rebellion, burning Rochester Cathedral. So, by a strange twist of fate, the sons of the despised pagan Penda had become devout Christian kings of Mercia, and overlords of all southern England.

21. Celtic Christianity Was Betrayed With a Smile

Oswy's wife, Queen Eanfled, was a follower of the Roman form of Christianity, whereas the king himself was of the Irish Celtic persuasion. This arrangement proved highly inconvenient because the two forms of Church celebrated Easter on different dates. This meant that while one part of the royal household was feasting the other half was fasting. The Irish-influenced monks wore their hair bared across the scalp, but the Romans wore theirs in a coronal fringe. A young monk called Wilfred had spent time in Lyons and Rome itself, where he had been captivated by the splendid display and elaborate ritual of the Roman Church. As the new abbot of Ripon he had the ear of the queen and in 663 Oswy was persuaded to preside over the convocation of a synod at Whitby to thrash out these irritating matters once and for all.

The bishop of Lindisfarne, Colman, put the Irish/Celtic case in simple terms. St Columba himself had done things in their way and he was a saint with God in heaven. King Oswy had been protected and tutored by the monks on Iona, and his kingdom had been saved by the efforts of the humble Aedan. There was no more to be said. Wilfred, who put the opposition case for Rome, presented a detailed and learned case. He had studied canon law and this maintained the primacy of the Holy See of Rome. The computations used by the Irish to calculate the date of Easter were, he claimed, erroneous and out of date, but his concluding argument was most telling of all. He subtly mocked the piety and simplicity of the Celtic monks and of their founder, Columba. To know the claims of primacy of the Holy See and to nevertheless ignore them was nothing less than sin. He appealed to Oswy and asked whether he would remain true to the faith of Columba, a simple ascetic monk who had dwelt at the edge of the world in a windswept monastery, or follow the apostolic succession of Rome, and its founder, St Peter, who had been appointed as leader of the Church by Christ himself? Oswy looked at Colman and smiled. He said he did not wish to get to the gates of heaven one day only to find that he had offended the man who held the keys, St Peter. This great divide in religion endured for many generations and was the most important ecclesiastical decision of the times. Wilfred became enormously powerful and wealthy, lavishing his new-found prosperity on building some of the most impressive monasteries in Europe. But for the Celtic party it was an irrevocable defeat from which they never really recovered.

22. AN AFRICAN REFUGEE HELPED TO REFORM THE ANGLO-SAXON CHURCH

As we have seen, it did not help that the Christian message was mediated by two different Churches, and so in the countryside people continued their folk traditions or intermingled them with a garbled form of Christianity. The word 'pagan' literally means 'a rustic', one who lived in the country areas that had been hardly penetrated by the Christian clergy. The motive for the conversion of the Anglo-Saxon kings was simple. They were told that the Christian God would bring them victory in war. It sometimes happened, however, that the Lord of Hosts didn't deliver, and so it only took a defeat in battle or the death of a king to undo everything the Christian missionaries had achieved.

The two most powerful Christian kings, Oswy of Northumbria and Egbert of Kent, selected a candidate they approved to be Archbishop of Canterbury, Wigheard, and sent him off to Rome. However, before he could receive his pallium from Pope Vitalian, Wigheard died, probably as a result of his exertions in getting to Rome. The Pope was in a dilemma. He knew how precarious and shallow the Christian mission was in England, and that it was sorely lacking in serious intellectual and theological discipline. He decided to offer the job to a young man, Hadrian 'the African', a refugee from North Africa whose talents had elevated him to the office of abbot at the age of only thirty. Hadrian declined, thinking it a job for an older, wiser man. Instead, the Pope offered the job to Theodore of Tarsus, an elderly Greek from what is now Turkey. He asked Hadrian to accompany Theodore on the arduous journey through France, where Hadrian had influential contacts. Hadrian accepted this supportive role and after a year the two unlikely companions arrived in England after many adventures. The duo set about their work with a will, and began to instruct the English clergy in Latin and Greek, as well as introducing music and geometry and sophisticated medical knowledge. One of Theodore's first acts was to summon the Bishop of Northumbria, Chad, to admonish him. Wilfred had originally been proposed as bishop of the region but had travelled to France to be consecrated. Whilst he was away Oswy chose Chad and had consecrated him instead. This was just the sort of thing Theodore had been sent to sort out and he demanded an explanation from Chad for this irregularity. Instead of arguing, Chad, who had been schooled in the Irish/Celtic tradition, immediately offered to resign, saying he had never considered himself worthy of the post in the first place. He retired to Lastingham in Yorkshire to become a simple hermit. Theodore had never seen such humility and simplicity and was immediately won over. He restored Wilfred, but made Chad Bishop of Mercia at Lichfield, where he founded the See in 669. Chad was so humble that he refused to ride a horse and when Theodore gave him one, personally hoisting him into the saddle, he later gave it away! Theodore lived to be eighty-eight, a grand old age in those days; Hadrian outlived him and also lived to be a great age, a refugee from Africa who died in England.

23. England Was a Mercian Concept

In the preceding fact I mentioned 'England' and 'the English Church' as if by now we had reached a stage where the Anglo-Saxons understood themselves to be in some sense one people, the 'English'. This lay many years in the future, but such a dawning realisation was just beginning, something they called *'Engla-lond'* or a homeland of the English. Why wasn't it called 'Saxon-land'? After all, the arrival of the Saxons on the island probably preceded that of the Angles, chronologically speaking. It may be that this was because the continental Saxons were still pagan at this time and the English wished to particularly differentiate themselves from this cruel, heathen folk. By contrast the Anglo-Saxons, although they were late-comers to Christianity, had become one of the leading bastions of the Church. A Devon man called Wynfrith (renamed 'Boniface' by Pope Gregory II) became the Apostle of the Germans and Frisians. He was eventually murdered by Frisian bandits, but thanks to his efforts the Christian message reached deep inside Germany. Another by-product of the Anglo-Saxon conversion was the proliferation of written charters. In one of these, the Ismere Diploma of 736, a king called Aethelbald of Mercia proclaims himself 'king of all the southern English'. Later in his reign he goes further and calls himself simply 'King of the English'. As early as 673 Archbishop Theodore had convoked the Synod of Hertford, which has been called 'the first constitutional measure of the collective English race'. Aethelbald was impressed by this example of different bishops subordinating themselves to one archbishop, and he took it as a model. By now the petty regional kings of sub-kingdoms such as the *Hwicce* or *Magonsaetan* had been reduced to a considerably inferior status to the king called 'ealdormen'. It seemed to him that the kings of Sussex, Kent, East Anglia, even Wessex, could be treated in a similar fashion and effectively demoted, but this was a policy which caused great resentment.

24. London Was a Thriving Trading Port

By the mid-eighth century King Aethelbald of Mercia had established overlordship of Middlesex and the area around London. The Anglo-Saxons originally abhorred cities and the Roman ruins of London lay largely deserted within its mighty walls, but nearby there was a riverside trading station called *Lundenwic* that did brisk business in luxury goods. Aethelbald had his eye on the tolls he could collect from this busy centre, and since Mercia was far from the coast, where most of the *wics* or small trading ports were located, London became vital to Mercia's economy and international influence. These tiny trading stations grew exponentially: *Eoferwic* (York) *Hamwic(h)* (Southampton) and Ipswich grew up to facilitate elite luxury trade. Although for the ordinary Anglo-Saxon the world outside the island was barely known, for the royalty and the elite in society there was contact with foreign people and a desire to import their goods. Bede describes London as a 'market for many people who come by land and sea' in 731. But this London was actually outside the massive Roman city walls (which remained standing for centuries) and located a mile away in what is now Aldwych, 'the old trading port'. It was not until Alfred took control of the city that it was re-located within the city walls as a defence against the Vikings. London remained in the Mercian sphere of influence until the reign of Edward the Elder.

25. A Mighty Mercian King Made His Mark

Aethelbald's long reign (forty-one years) had established Mercia as the foremost Anglo-Saxon nation. He was murdered by his own bodyguards at Seckington near Tamworth while he lay sleeping and for a while the succession was disputed. Offa, who eventually prevailed in the civil war that followed, became a ruler with an international reputation, and he is one of the few Anglo-Saxon kings most modern people will have heard of. The reason for his enduring fame is the famous landmark he caused to be built, a 149-mile-long dyke dividing English from Welsh territory that is still plainly visible along much of its length today, one of the engineering wonders of the age.

If some modern historians debate the origins of the dyke, the Welsh are in little doubt. They call the work *Clawdd Offa*. In places it was defended by a ditch and bank twenty-five feet from bottom to top surmounted by a wooden palisade. Along the length there were occasional watchtowers and possibly a line of stacked beacons to alert patrols to any intruders. There were regular controlled entrance gates to facilitate peaceful drovers and traders or churchmen or diplomats, but the prospect of rustling large herds of fat English cattle over the border was now a thing of the past. It was unfortunate but many Anglo-Saxon villages found themselves on the wrong side of the dyke, which is not exactly coterminous with the border. The construction gangs were drawn from all over England, not just Mercia, and they had been summoned under a levy known as *burhbot*. This was similar to military service, except for the fact that men came with buckets and shovels instead of spears and shields to repair roads or build forts, but nothing on this scale had ever been known in Anglo-Saxon history. The project to build the dyke involved all Anglo-Saxons who owed fealty to Offa and put paid to any doubts about his authority. He soon showed the whole world who was in charge in *Engla-lond*. Thousands of labourers and engineers cut and raised the dyke in the space of a year or so, cutting a swathe from Basingwerk near Prestatyn in north Wales. It is possible that Offa got the idea from his namesake, Offa of Angeln, the distant ancestor of the Mercian kings in their original homelands. He had 'fixed the boundary against the Myrgings of Fifledor', according to an ancient saga. But there was another reason behind the project. Offa (rather foolishly) thought of himself as the English equivalent of the Frankish emperor, Charlemagne. Charlemagne had a scheme by which he hoped to excavate a canal between the Rhine and the Danube, but the project was so immense that it had to be abandoned. Was Offa 'cocking a snook' at his Frankish rival?

26. Offa Was an Empire Builder

The Mercian royal house had asserted its dominion over the confederacy of tribes which acknowledged Mercian overlordship by gradually subordinating sub-kings of small tribal regions, giving them the title of 'ealdorman', a class of nobility considerably inferior to the king. This solution coloured Offa's ideas about how the kings of the subordinate realms in the south, like Wessex, Sussex, and Kent, should fit into his vision for *Engla-lond*. It was one thing to force the kings of the *Hwicce* to demote themselves, but it was quite another to expect kings of proud nations like Wessex or Kent to do so. Offa's early years were spent in constant warfare to keep the lower-ranking kingdoms in line and his methods were probably not so very different from those used by a heathen like Penda in his day. One of the most remarkable things about Offa is that he seems almost the embodiment of the transition from post-Roman barbarism, represented by Penda, to a confident, outward-looking, wealthy and respectable Anglo-Saxon polity which began to emerge during his later years. There was much more to Offa than 'Offa's Dyke', as we will see, and what he wanted most of all was to establish Mercia as a respected leader among all the Anglo-Saxon peoples.

As a relative latecomer to the civilised world, Mercia was still backward and its power had been exerted solely by virtue of armed might. When Sussex rebelled against him Offa put down the uprising with typical ruthlessness, but when Kent did the same thing four years later Offa failed to put down their rebellion. Possibly to repair his damaged prestige, Offa invaded Wales and then Wessex, opening the way for him to attempt another campaign against Kent. After thirty years on the throne, in 787 Offa decided to stage a grand ceremony, a jubilee to celebrate his long reign, but also to have his son, Ecgfrith, consecrated as a king. Offa was taking no chances, and with his enemies cowed he prepared for a display of pomp and imperial majesty to rival that of any court in Europe.

27. Offa Offended the Most Powerful Man in Europe

In Offa's time, all of Europe looked up to Charlemagne, the greatest Christian ruler since the collapse of the Roman Empire. Offa managed to annoy him, potentially a very serious mistake! Charlemagne doted on his daughters and his favourite was Bertha. He had no problem in arranging prestige marriages for his sons and it was a great honour that Offa's daughter, Aelflaed, was accepted to become the bride of Charles, Charlemagne's son, but Offa was not content with this. In Charlemagne's eyes Offa was a petty little king of a backward country on a small island. It came as a shock when Offa stated that he would only approve his daughter's marriage if Ecgfrith, his precious son, should take Bertha, Charlemagne's spoiled and wilful daughter, as his wife. Charlemagne was absolutely incensed. He ordered his ports to be closed to all English ships and broke off diplomatic contacts. Various English exiles were sheltering from Offa at Charlemagne's court and they began to poison his mind against Offa. Offa's grand pretensions to international eminence had backfired in style.

Damage limitation was the order of the day. The sanctions Charlemagne imposed were designed to be a 'slap on the wrist' for Offa to let him know who was boss, but in truth no one wanted a stand-off between England and mainland Europe. When tempers had cooled Offa showed his contrition by endowing Frankish monasteries and soon the incident was forgotten. It was important to Charlemagne to assert his leadership as the saviour of Christianity, and Offa was a Christian brother, a man after his own heart. Offa had requested quern-stones ('black stones') for revolutionary mills which were appearing in the new towns and settlements he was developing, and Charlemagne was happy to oblige, providing that Offa ensured that English woollen cloaks and blankets were provided which were of a standardised size. Charlemagne sent rich gifts of silken vestments for all the bishops in England, but there was a special gift for Offa. When the 'Ring of the Avars', the gigantic fortress of the Asiatic hordes, had been stormed by his armies, vast booty and treasures had been taken. One of the prizes was an Avar sword, a cavalry sabre in a gilded bejewelled sheath. This was sent as a gift to Offa, and was so jealously guarded that it passed down from one English king to the next until the eleventh century.

28. A Holy Pilgrim Became a Reviled Murderer

Once his quarrels with Charlemagne had blown over, Offa set out on a pilgrimage to Rome in 792. No doubt he felt very proud as he processed through Francia and Italy accompanied by a splendid retinue. People there would have known little about him. No Anglo-Saxon king had ever established such a reputation abroad, and to the awestruck onlookers he was simply 'the King of the English'. So why does he not stand as high in the regard of modern Englishmen today as say, Alfred the Great or Athelstan? The answer lies in his conflicted character. Offa was not a man people loved, but many people feared him, with good cause. As Alcuin of York, Charlemagne's chief advisor, wrote, he was 'a man stained with blood'. To others he was a parvenu and a bully, and one final evil act sullied his reputation beyond hope of repair.

Aethelberht II of East Anglia decided to issue coins which bore his own image, perhaps as a sign that he no longer recognised Offa as his overlord. It was a fatal mistake. In May 794 Aethelberht was summoned to meet Offa at Sutton Walls, one of his palaces in Herefordshire. He was bound and taken to a nearby stream by Grimbert, Offa's henchman, where he was beheaded. The body was taken away to be disposed of, but in legend, the head fell off the cart and restored a blind man's sight. Regicide was a crime against God in the eyes of the common folk and Aethelberht became a saint. Everyone knew who had ordered the foul deed and even in Mercia itself people were revolted. When Offa died in July 796 at Offley in Hertfordshire, aged over sixty, it must have seemed that Mercian supremacy was assured. Ecgfrith succeeded him but died later that year, within months of his father, leaving no heirs. Alcuin was not alone in thinking this a punishment from God on Offa and his line, and by implication on Mercia itself. Offa had reigned for thirty-nine years and his achievements speak for themselves, but he was not remembered with affection by all Anglo-Saxons. The subordinated kings of the south, Sussex, Kent and even Wessex, resented Mercian overlordship and never accepted their demotion to the status of client-kingdoms. Offa was greedy, arrogant, ruthless and cruel, despite an outward show of piety and generosity to the Church. Nevertheless, among his own countrymen, the Mercians, he is still called 'Offa the Great'. He was the greatest of their rulers without any doubt, and thanks to his efforts a process was initiated which would, one day, bring about a united England.

29. January Was 'The Wolf Month'

The England inhabited by the Anglo-Saxons was a very different country to the one we are used to today. The population was small and widely dispersed in self-contained communities. Of the entire population (between 1 and 2 million people) less than 10 per cent lived in settlements we would recognise as towns. The endless backbreaking toil in the fields tied people to their villages and most people hardly ever left their community in their entire lifetime. The great forests were a vital resource, both for the carefully cultivated harvest of timber for building materials and for feeding the swine on 'pannage', beech-mast, acorns and the like. This ensured a steady supply of pork, the most readily available meat supply. The forests and marshes were home to all sorts of animals which are now extinct in Britain, such as roe deer, beavers and (until they were recently reintroduced) wild boar. But there was one beast which haunted the Anglo-Saxon imagination like no other – the wolf. The social disintegration and depopulation which followed the end of Roman Britain probably led to an increase in the wolf population and they were a menace to small farmers with livestock, particularly in the cold winter months. The Anglo-Saxons called January 'the wolf month', when the howling packs became reckless through hunger and would dare attacks on the sheepfolds and cattle stalls. Because people lived (quite literally) with their animals, and knew each by sight, confrontation with the ravenous wolves, who would even attack horses or bulls, was inevitable. Although attacks on humans were rare, they were not unheard of; many a tale of gigantic monstrous wolves must have been told around the mid-winter hearths, only adding to their bad reputation. Wolves were a menace all through the period we are considering and active measures were taken to exterminate them.

During the reign of King Athelstan in the tenth century wolves were so prevalent in Flixton, Yorkshire, that a special compound had to be erected there as a refuge for travellers (people travelling alone were most vulnerable of all). The Welsh border country was infested with wolves and eventually King Edgar attempted to eradicate the threat by commuting money payments Athelstan had levied as tribute on the Welsh princes, and instead asked for an annual tally of 300 wolf heads. The statement that Edgar extirpated the wolves in England was part of the laudatory propaganda which remembered him as 'Edgar the Peaceful'. In fact, wolves survived for many centuries more, and there is evidence of organised wolf hunts in Staffordshire, Shropshire, Gloucestershire, Herefordshire and Worcestershire taking place hundreds of years later.

30. A Mutilated King Died in a Monastery

Ecgfrith had died childless so the crown of Mercia passed to Coenwulf, a son of one of Offa's cousins called Cuthbert. Mercian supremacy was by no means at an end, but its nature had changed. As soon as the satellite kingdoms showed signs of rebelliousness Coenwulf put them in their place with a ruthlessness that surpassed even Offa's grim reputation. He called himself 'Emperor of Britain' and intended to impose Mercian domination by armed force. To show he meant business he embarked on a campaign in Wales which devastated the entire country, taking vast booty. The 'Mercian incendiaries', as the Welsh called them, left Wales as a blackened wasteland but Coenwulf was quite prepared to adopt this strategy against other Anglo-Saxon kingdoms. When a monk, Eadberht Praen, who had been in exile with Charlemagne, returned to claim the throne of Kent Coenwulf retaliated by invading, where he unleashed an orgy of destruction, driving the population into the desolate Romney Marsh. Eadberht Praen was captured, blinded and had his hands chopped off before being taken in chains back into Mercia. There is folklore to suggest that he survived, and was taken into the care of his fellow monks at Winchcombe Abbey in Gloucestershire, where he eventually died some years later. Such sickening brutality did not endear Coenwulf to the Pope, Leo III, and Coenwulf's request to have the whole of England placed under one archbishopric at London was denied. Lichfield soon lost its status as an archbishopric and from then on Mercia's decline as the foremost Anglo-Saxon power was assured.

31. TERRIBLE OMENS FORETOLD DISASTER

The Christianity of the Anglo-Saxons was very different from ours today. They were illiterate, even most kings could not read and write and the clergy were only a little more advanced in intellectual or scientific matters. God had set the stars in their stations at the beginning of time and so comets, which appeared for a while only to disappear just as mysteriously, were inexplicable, unless God was angry with them, or worse, Satan had unleashed his demons to plague them. When King Edgar died in 975 a comet appeared shortly afterwards and within the year a terrible famine ravaged England. In April 1066 another comet appeared, and we all know what that portended! When Ethelred 'the Unready', the most infamous king in Anglo-Saxon history, was consecrated king in 979 a 'bloody welkin', a shimmering blood-red cloud, enveloped the kingdom at night and disappeared in the mornings. Probably this was a rare apparition of the Northern Lights but the simple people, or indeed the superstitious clergy, did not know this. In 995 another comet appeared just as the Danes returned to devastate the entire country.

The *Anglo-Saxon Chronicle* relates that in 793,

Dreadful forewarnings came over the land of the Northumbrians, terrifying the people most woefully ... immense sheets of lightning rushing through the air, and whirlwinds, and fiery dragons flying across the firmament. These tremendous tokens were soon followed by a great famine; and not long after, on the sixth day before the ides of January in the same year, the harrowing inroads of heathen men made lamentable havoc in the church of God in Holy Island (Lindisfarne), by rapine and slaughter.

The sacred monastery at Lindisfarne, the epicentre of English Christian life, had been attacked by Scandinavian raiders and for the first time the Anglo-Saxons faced a threat from outside the island. The strange signs in the heavens did indeed warn of a grim time of trial, an ordeal which was to change the Anglo-Saxon way of life irrevocably in the coming centuries. The terrifying Vikings had arrived.

32. The Vikings Were Like a Throwback to the Original Anglo-Saxons

Like the original Anglo-Saxons the Vikings worshipped gods like Woden, who they called 'Odin'. Their languages at this time were closely related, but the Vikings would have spoken with a broad dialect. It has proven almost impossible to distinguish their DNA traces in most of England from their Anglo-Saxon neighbours. Their motives in coming to England were the same too: raiding and plunder, and then when opportunity allowed, invasion and conquest. Their appearance in 793 was the beginning of a long relationship between the two peoples which, shall we say, had its 'ups and downs' but the tendency to stress their positive qualities in recent years should not hide the fact that the Anglo-Saxons (and others) saw the Vikings as almost demonic terrorists, a punishment from God for their sins.

Their great advantage lay in surprise, and their shallow-draught clinker built longships could arrive anywhere, using the estuaries and mouths of rivers as gateways into the hinterland. Each of these superbly designed and expertly built craft carried up to forty fully armed warriors. Their legendary seamanship took them deep into the Eurasian interior, the Mediterranean, across the Atlantic Ocean to North America and over all of Western Europe. These formidable adversaries, following the traditional sea lanes around the British Isles, soon realised that Anglo-Saxon England, plagued by its divided kingdoms, was theirs for the taking, and it was upon them that their heaviest and most sustained blows were to fall in the decades to come. The Vikings were fanatical about war, and like modern suicide bombers they were eager for a glorious death in battle, so much so that they would strip naked and don the skins of bears or wolves (respectively called *Berserkers* or *Ulfhednars*) and career into the shield wall of the enemy snarling and biting, their eyes rolling in their heads, frothing at the mouth. This cultural stereotype of the Vikings is deeply imprinted on western culture, but of course there was a lot more to them than that, as we shall see, but for the Anglo-Saxons it must have seemed as if the ghosts of their pagan ancestors had come back to haunt them.

33. A Three-Day-Old Baby Became a Saint

The Anglo-Saxons were as obsessed by their saints as we are by television celebrities, popstars and sports heroes. The new parish churches that were being built all contained purported relics of one saint or another. One reason why the Viking incursions came as such a shock to them was because the very foundation of their culture, their religion, was the main target for the pirates. This was not just because of a possible dislike for Christianity as we saw earlier, but because monasteries and religious houses had a subsidiary function as modern banks; they were the safety-deposit boxes of their times. They also contained books, which were so extremely rare and valuable that they could be ransomed. As the churches and monasteries and libraries burned, the cultural and intellectual life of the Anglo-Saxons was eroded almost to extinction, but they did not become less religious, indeed more so, their rationale being that they were generating sin which God was punishing them for in the shape of the Northmen.

Saints came in all shapes and sizes and were not always of exotic origin. In fact, the Anglo-Saxons had many home-grown saints; some were even murdered kings like St Aethelberht or St Kenelm. In fact, they proliferated to such an extent that, following the Norman Conquest, the newly installed Italian Archbishop of Canterbury, Lanfranc, ordered that English holy relics should be put to the test, lest they prove fraudulent. The supreme Anglo-Saxon saint was King Edmund of East Anglia, and he was one of the many martyrs the English venerated. We will look at King Edmund's story a little later on, but perhaps the strangest of all the Anglo-Saxon saints was St Rumbold. He was supposed to have been a grandson of Penda who was born in the 660s in King's Sutton in Northamptonshire. Miraculously he was born with the ability to speak, and after declaring himself a faithful Christian he asked for baptism and communion. He then gave a lengthy sermon quoting extensively from the Bible before announcing that he would soon die, and after three days he did so, probably the youngest saint in history!

It was no accident that there was a strong link between Anglo-Saxon royalty and saintliness. Remember how the Anglo-Saxons thought that their kings and queens were literally divine? When they became Christians they simply transferred this cult of royal divinity onto the Christian faith. One typical such saint was St Guthlac. He was a kinsman of the Mercian kings and had become a soldier aged only fifteen. Warfare was brutal and by the time he was twenty-four Guthlac felt the need to retire to a monastery at Repton to ease his troubled conscience. He was not popular among the monks there and soon left to become a hermit in the fenlands of Cambridgeshire. He was shown a lonely island in the stinking marshes where he lived a life of asceticism, drinking muddy bog water and eating dry bread. In his day the marshes were the refuge of the last British-speakers, and they tried to drive him away from the place, uttering curses and conjuring demons with ghastly twisted faces, horses' teeth, and deformed limbs, vomiting flames out of their mouths. Perhaps some of the bread Guthlac had eaten was 'crazy bread' infected with the hallucinogenic fungus ergot, which gave people visions known as St Anthony's Fire?

34. Wessex Emerged as the Most Powerful English Kingdom

The King of Wessex, Egbert, had been in exile at Charlemagne's court in Francia while a Mercian puppet king ruled in his stead. In 825 a decisive battle called *Ellandun* took place outside Swindon between Egbert and Beornwulf of Mercia and it was a resounding West Saxon victory. Not only was the independence of Wessex re-established, but all the southern kingdoms, Sussex, Kent, Essex and the region of Surrey, accepted Egbert's overlordship. Egbert moved against the Celts of Cornwall and subdued them before invading Mercia and compelling Northumbria to pay tribute to him. Egbert became the new *Bretwalda*, the 'wide ruler' or high king of England. We have seen how the centre of political gravity had been moving from north to south for centuries, from Northumbria to Mercia and now, finally, to Wessex. It had taken a long time but at last the descendants of Cerdic could claim supremacy. Ironically, just as the Anglo-Saxons seemed to be uniting as one nation under a pre-eminent royal dynasty, the 'England' they had striven for so long to build was about to collapse around them. In 832 the Vikings took control of the Isle of Sheppey and in the same year Egbert attacked a shipload of pirates at Charmouth. The mighty king was repulsed with heavy losses. He died in 836 and his son Aethelwulf succeeded him at a time when the Viking raids were intensifying. The early years of his reign all report heavy Danish raids. It was not just Wessex which endured these ceaseless attacks. The Anglo-Saxons now realised belatedly that they would have to do something completely alien to them if they were going to survive – they were going to have to cooperate.

In 853 a large Viking fleet landed in Anglesey under a chieftain called Orm. Gwynedd was ravaged and then the Viking army raided into Powys, whose king immediately fled the country and exiled himself to far-off Rome. Burgred, the king of Mercia, desperately looked around for allies, especially to King Aethelwulf of Wessex, but the latter was away on a pilgrimage to Rome and could not help. Fortunately the Welsh kings did unite. They expelled the Vikings and slew Orm, but the writing was now on the wall for Mercia.

35. A 'GREAT ARMY' DESTROYED THREE ANGLO-SAXON KINGDOMS

In 865 a huge fleet of Viking ships landed thousands of warriors on the East Anglian coast. The time for raiding was over; now the Vikings had come to stay. Two kings called Ivar and Halfdan, the sons of a chieftain called Ragnar Lothbrok, rounded up the best horses they could find and proceeded to pillage the area. In 867 they moved on to York where they set up a puppet king. The next year the *micel here* or 'Great Army' of the Vikings, as it was called, tried their luck in Mercia. By now the terrorist tactics of the Vikings had begun to unman the Anglo-Saxon kings. It was scarcely surprising, for the speciality of Ivar 'the Boneless' was a ritual execution known as 'the blood-eagle', whereby the victim's ribs and lungs were eviscerated by making an incision down the backbone, and then splayed out so that they looked like an eagle's wings. This had been the fate of Aelle of Northumbria, the quisling ruler who had defected to the Vikings, only to rebel against them. His fate must have been very much in the mind of Burgred, the King of Mercia, for the Viking Great Army had invaded his territory and ensconced themselves at Nottingham.

Burgred had accepted Mercia's diminished power and as early as 853 he had carried out a joint invasion of Wales with the West Saxon king, Aethelwulf. The Mercians and West Saxons had adopted a virtually identical currency and had agreed to put each other's troops at the disposal of either threatened party. All this was eminently practical but it came too late. Burgred requested the new King of Wessex, Aethelred, and his younger brother Alfred, to come to his aid in besieging Nottingham, refortified by the Vikings with strong new defences. It proved impossible to breach these and the allied English army broke off the siege. The Mercians were forced to pay the Danes to depart north to York again. These perambulations had the effect of unnerving and demoralising the whole Anglo-Saxon population, for the contract between a king and his people was that they worked hard and paid their taxes to the noblemen and the king and tithes to the Church in exchange for their protection against foreign enemies. The Vikings seemed able to behave with apparent impunity, and even when they were brought to battle, as often as not they prevailed. What the Anglo-Saxons needed was a king whom God clearly favoured, a man marked out as the one destined to deliver them from their enemies.

36. AN ANGLO-SAXON KING BECAME THE NATIONAL SAINT

In the space of a few short years, three Anglo-Saxon kingdoms, Northumbria, East Anglia, and Mercia, were destroyed. In 869 the Vikings invaded East Anglia. On 20 November the young East Anglian king, Edmund, offered them battle outside Thetford and was soundly beaten. He escaped to a wood called *Haeglesdune* near Hoxne before being discovered by Viking outriders. Edmund was dragged to a tree (later called 'Edmund's Oak') where he was bound, scourged and used as target practice for Danish archers until the arrows protruded from his body like 'the spines of a hedge-hog'. He was then impaled, cut down and suffered the gory ordeal of the 'blood-eagle'. As a final insult he was decapitated and his head casually discarded by being thrown into a thorn-thicket. When his head and body were found and reunited, they were discovered to be incorruptible, a sure sign of saintliness. He became venerated as the national saint of the entire Anglo-Saxon people. The Great Army moved on to *Medeshamstede* (modern Peterborough) where they pillaged the magnificent abbey before deciding to try their luck in Wessex, where after vicious fighting they were expelled in 871. The *micel here* returned to Northumbria before finally establishing themselves at Repton in Mercia. The writing was on the wall. Burgred was not going to suffer Edmund's fate and fled to Rome where he died in ignominious exile in 888. Now only one Anglo-Saxon kingdom remained unoccupied by the Vikings, Wessex.

The Anglo-Saxons, though, were to be no pushover. They were a tough and warlike people but they needed leaders who could inspire the underlying martial traditions held sacred by their illustrious ancestors. Edmund had become a saint, but he had lost his kingdom. What was needed now was an ordinary man, not a saint, who won battles rather than lost them. Fortunately for them, Wessex had finally emerged as the most powerful Anglo-Saxon realm under a line of kings who took great care to nurture strong martial traditions and husbanded their wealth, even if that meant offending the Church. The Vikings were about to meet their match. In 870, during a cold winter, they struck their blow. They occupied a site outside Reading and fortified it. This time they were immediately opposed. The West Saxons did not dither to wait around for their king, Aethelred, but rallied to the local ealdorman, Aethelwulf, who immediately cut off and slaughtered Viking foraging parties. The Vikings retired behind their impregnable defences until eventually King Aethelred and his brother, Alfred, arrived to besiege them. It was virtually impossible to storm a Viking fort and so the West Saxon army retired, going home to celebrate Christmas, but the prospects for the coming year must have seemed very bleak!

37. The Feast Was at the Centre of Community Life

We have all seen cinematic representations of medieval feasts, and although those who enjoyed the celebrations were from the upper echelons, nobility, churchmen and of course the kings, they were the focus for the entire community. Kings could not afford to live in one place all of the time but were peripatetic, travelling around the country with large retinues of soldiers, servants, stewards, and family members, all of whom needed feeding! It must have been a nightmare when the king's messenger arrived to inform you that this travelling circus was on its way to your hall, for it was likely to cost you dearly, one way or the other. These entertainments needed extensive and careful planning and meticulous preparation. The first thing to check was that the ale was freshly brewed. There were no hops, so ale went sour quickly and had to be drunk fresh, and the Anglo-Saxons were (some would say still are) notoriously thirsty! A special and much more potent drink was mead, which was brewed using honeycombs. Not only was it exceptionally potent in alcohol, but it had the virtue of being sweet in a world without sugar. The nobility also imported wine, but this was of poor quality and inferior potency compared to wine nowadays.

A typical royal feast for one evening might have included fifty casks of ale, a couple of roast oxen, 300 flat breads (which served as a rough platter) twenty chickens, ten geese, five salmon, 100 eels, a dozen jars of honey, a cask of butter, a dozen cheeses and perhaps other delicacies such as pike, or even a porpoise! To ensure a steady supply of all this it was necessary to introduce an organised production of food tributes under the scrutiny of kings' stewards called the *feorm*, from which we derive our word 'farm'. Then, when all were replete the music and storytelling would commence. The *Scop* (pronounced 'shop') was the professional entertainer, historian, comedian, but most crucially, the musician. Music was revered as a kind of magic which had power to heal (or to harm) living people, and everyone was expected to 'take a turn' at playing the lyre or harp as it passed down the mead-benches. The Anglo-Saxon saint Caedmon was so embarrassed at being unable to sing a song at a community gathering that he retired in misery, unable to face his peers. Fortunately, that evening an angel came to him in a dream, and gave him a song of such wondrous beauty that he became a saint, a celebrity pop-idol of his day! Huge fires ensured warmth and conviviality, even in the long dark winters, when people would stare into the flames as they heard the sagas being recounted, deep in concentration – after all, the word 'focus' was originally the Latin for 'a hearth'!

38. A Small Boy Won a Rich Prize

In 849 a child was born at Wantage in Berkshire, a boy who was to become England's greatest king, Alfred. It was a miracle that he became a king at all, as he had three older brothers. There are many myths and tales about him – we all know the one about the cakes! Not all of these are 'facts' but they should not all be discounted. This was a medieval 'superman' whose incredible life cannot be easily distilled into a few facts.

When he was just four years old something unusual happened to him. His father sent a delegation to the Pope in Rome and the embassy included his youngest son, Alfred, who was invested with an honorific consulship. This ceremony closely resembled the coronation anointing of Anglo-Saxon kings, and despite his being so far back in line from the throne it was thought that he had been marked out by God as a special kind of king. There was something special about Alfred.

When he had returned from Rome (a very arduous and very exciting journey for one so young) he returned to the 'real world' of Anglo-Saxon Wessex and the bosom of his close and loving family. His mother, Queen Osburga, doted on her children and inculcated a love of literature, religion and art. One day she called the boys together and showed them a beautifully illuminated book. Books were rare and treasured, considered the preserve of the elite class and the Church. The book was a compendium of Anglo-Saxon poetry, stories which contained the most elemental themes of Anglo-Saxon consciousness. The child who could learn it by heart should have the book as a prize. None of the boys could read, of course, and the three other boys were older and best placed to prepare for the task of reciting it. On the day of reckoning it was the youngest, Alfred, who won the book. He had gone to a monk and meticulously prepared, hearing the lines read out over and over again until he knew each poem word-perfect. This determination and the ability to concentrate his mind on the matter in hand is a strong theme in the biography that was written about Alfred by Bishop Asser, a Welshman recruited by Alfred to rebuild learning in his devastated kingdom. By the time he married Ealhswith, his Mercian bride, when he was twenty, Alfred was a respected and powerful prince, but not yet a king.

39. Alfred's Quick Thinking Saved the Day

As we have seen, Wessex was not immune from the Viking threat. In 871 they invaded Wessex and established themselves behind impenetrable defences at Reading but their foraging parties rode into Ealdorman Aethelwulf, one of King Aethelred's local commanders. Ealdorman Aethelwulf was killed in the assault on Reading. As soon as the West Saxon army fell back they were pursued by the Vikings as far as Ashdown on the ancient Ridgeway and here, around a stunted thorn tree, a vicious battle was fought. The king was celebrating Mass as the battle commenced, refusing to leave until the ceremony was completed. This piety almost cost him his kingdom, but fortunately Alfred took a more practical view and led the West Saxons against the foe in a furious charge up the steep downs. Around the thorn tree an epic struggle went on all morning before finally Aethelred arrived with his own household troops to turn the tide. By then Alfred had inflicted terrible casualties on the Vikings, leaving a king and five *jarls* dead and many thousands killed or wounded.

Unfortunately this early pressure failed to dislodge the enemy. At Basing the Vikings defeated Aethelred and Alfred, and a hard fought battle at Marden also ended with a West Saxon defeat. At this point Aethelred died, and as Alfred was attending his brother's funeral news came that the Vikings were on the move again, now reinforced by a vast new army. It was obvious that Aethelred's young sons would have to be overlooked in this national emergency and Alfred was chosen as the new King of Wessex by a unanimous vote.

Unfortunately, not even Alfred's efforts would prove sufficient to dislodge the Great Army. At the Battle of Wilton his army was beaten decisively and after nine large battles and hundreds of smaller skirmishes in a year the West Saxon army was exhausted. Alfred was forced to accept the inevitable. He ordered the gathering of a tax known as the *gafol* or *geld* which was a levy payable on each hide of land. A hide was a measure of land sufficient to support one large extended family group. This tax was then paid to the Danes (the Vikings in England were almost all of Danish origins) to leave and go elsewhere, at least for a while. So it was not a good start for Alfred, but he had survived, and so had his kingdom. For a few years at least, the Danes left Wessex alone, concentrating their energies on destroying Mercia and consolidating their hold on Northumbria.

40. King Alfred Burned the Cakes

It seems likely that by now a network of Viking spies was active in England as the Viking leader Guthrum seems to have had intelligence that Alfred was to spend Christmas with his family at Chippenham in Wiltshire. Guthrum stole out of Gloucester and rode with a large force to Chippenham with the intention of taking Alfred alive. Alfred and a few faithful followers and his immediate family managed to escape in the nick of time. He was forced to flee to the impenetrable marshes of Somerset. Meanwhile, in the depths of winter the Vikings billeted themselves on the West Saxons. There was nothing for it but to capitulate and endure their depredations, except for the lucky few who managed to escape overseas. Alfred erected a fort on the 'island' of Athelney in the marshes but life there was literally hand to mouth. It proved necessary to emerge from hiding to raid Viking foraging parties to steal their food, but there was another unpleasant task to be undertaken. Any West Saxon household who gave shelter or comfort to the heathens (even though there was little else they could do) were considered traitors who must be brutally punished. It was in this miserable and dangerous time that the story of the 'cakes' took hold. We can perhaps understand how these tales began, for by now Alfred was a hunted desperado. Later, when the great king was entertaining in his mead hall, perhaps he told his listeners about the time when he had sought shelter in the hovel of a cowherd. The woman of the house, annoyed to have an unknown intruder hogging her fire, asked Alfred to watch that the scone cakes on a griddle on the hearth did not scorch, but Alfred was so intent on tending his bow and arrows that he forgot to heed her. The woman was furious and admonished the (disguised) king, reminding him that he would be quick enough to devour them when they were ready! There are many versions of the story, and for me it has a ring of truth which entitles it to be included as a 'fact', a self-deprecating modesty we might expect of a truly great man, but strangely enough some historians say that it is an old Viking folk-tale, grafted onto Alfred. What is for sure is that by this stage in his reign Alfred's position was extremely precarious, and that his kingdom had shrunk to a few miles of stinking bog-land. From being a mighty king, he had been reduced to enduring a nagging from a cowherd's irritated wife! His countrymen were not faring much better, and those with the wherewithal fled by sea, possibly to France. Alfred could not hide forever, and when spring came he prepared to take the greatest gamble of his life.

41. Alfred Returned to Win a Famous Victory

The Vikings had a rough idea of where Alfred was hiding and in 878 a fleet of twenty-three ships attempted a landing on the north Devon coast. Their ships were observed by scouts and the local ealdorman of Devon, Odda, rapidly assembled the county levies. The fight was desperate and the Vikings lost their magical banner, called 'the Raven', thought to ensure victory in every battle. 800 Vikings were slain. The psychological effect was electrifying. News of the battle spread like wildfire and the cowed and resentful population began to believe a comeback was possible. It is not precisely known how the West Saxon resistance was organised but it was extremely effective. Easter seems to have been a crucial time, symbolising resurrection, and within a few weeks the West Saxons were arming themselves. This was the crucial moment for Anglo-Saxon England. If the West Saxons failed, the Danes would become their *de facto* overlords. The mustering point was a place called 'Egbert's Stone' and at Whitsuntide, Alfred appeared before the jubilant fighting men of Hampshire, Somerset and Wiltshire, many of whom must have seriously doubted if he was still alive. The only thought in their minds was ruthless revenge upon the hated Danes and they rapidly marched to Edington on Salisbury Plain where Guthrum was encamped. Alfred led the attack 'in dense battle-order'. The result was a stunning West Saxon victory with thousands of Guthrum's men left dead on the field or hunted down as they sought safety in Chippenham. Those who managed to escape were starved into surrender after a fortnight. The tables were turned and now Guthrum and all his men lay at Alfred's mercy. What Alfred did next showed a magnanimous and statesmanlike command of the situation. After all he had endured, Alfred forgave them and spared them, if they promised to convert to Christianity, swearing solemn oaths. Alfred himself stood as godfather to Guthrum at his baptism and the two became 'friends and brothers', feasting and hunting and hawking together for some weeks. Eventually what was left of Guthrum's army moved on to Cirencester for a year before finally settling in East Anglia. What Alfred had realised, and which was an ineluctable fact, was that the Vikings could not now be dislodged from England, that in time more would come, and that one battle was not going to change that. The Vikings had learned something too. They had thought the Anglo-Saxons to be weak and effete, but Alfred had changed all that!

42. Alfred Was a Disabled Polymath

We have seen that Alfred was a man of many parts, but there is one aspect of his life which is often overlooked. Alfred was what we would call 'disabled'. He was always afflicted by various illnesses from his childhood, including piles, an especially painful condition for a young *Aetheling* or prince, who would have spent much of his time in the saddle! This embarrassing and draining illness was the least of his worries though. He suffered from some sort of illness (possibly Crohn's disease) which came on at some point during most days. Commonly such people distract themselves from their suffering by displacement activities and throwing themselves into their work, and perhaps this was what Alfred did.

We know about all this because a Welsh monk called Asser was invited to become a member of a 'think tank' gathered around Alfred at his court. The Vikings had virtually destroyed intellectual life in England and among his many other projects the king was determined to rebuild learning in his realm. Alfred was a town planner and initiated the building of many new towns, or *burhs* – fortified market towns. Towns that had been destroyed were rebuilt. Alfred is also called the 'father of the English navy'. He reformed the law codes of his country, ensuring efficient jurisdiction in his realm.

But there was one last supreme project which he took personal charge of which astonished Asser, and which still seems incredible today. He decided that he would revive the intellectual life of the great monastic centres by translating several important books 'most needful for men to know', books by outstanding theologians and philosophers of their day. He invented the 'candle-clock', candles which burned at a steady rate hour by hour marked by lines bearing numerals for the hour. The lantern, made of a candle placed in a box made of finely-planed transparent horn, gave a powerful light. The invention was in use until the industrial revolution. Copies of the king's books were sent out to all the great cathedral churches and monasteries as gifts, the idea being that the bishops should use them to instruct the barely literate parish clergy. It is not too much to say that he saved English civilisation from extinction by his own efforts. No wonder that he is the only English king called 'the Great', but what is more remarkable is that all this was achieved despite a gruelling struggle with a relentless disability.

43. England Was Divided into Two Halves

Guthrum or, as we should now call him, 'Athelstan' (the baptismal name he had taken), had kept his side of the bargain with Alfred, and his men became farmers in East Anglia where he ruled until he died in 890. This did not mean that the Vikings were no longer a threat, very far from it, but it did confirm Alfred's intuition that there was no prospect of eliminating them completely in the foreseeable future. In 886 Alfred had no choice but to formally accept the facts on the ground. Northumbria, East Anglia, and eastern Mercia were *de facto* Danish conquests and in the treaty, a copy of which survives at the University of Cambridge, a boundary was drawn which acknowledged the predominance of Danish law, customs and culture north of a line 'up the Thames and river Lea to its source, then to Bedford, then up the (river) Ouse to Watling Street'. Watling Street was the ancient Roman road which we have already looked at, connecting London to the vicinity of Chester. This did not mean that everyone north of this boundary was Danish. The mass of the population were still Anglo-Saxons and some Anglo-Britons, but a small and well-armed warrior aristocracy of Vikings were the overlords there. As a trading folk the Danes needed secure and easily accessible trading centres. The main such centre was York, but in the eastern Midlands they had also developed thriving bases at Nottingham, Derby, Lincoln, Stamford and Leicester, the so called 'five boroughs'. The Danish-controlled area became known as the 'Danelaw'.

There was one centre which mattered above all others, London, but London was not a West Saxon city, and was still technically in Mercia. Alfred wanted the western Mercians to become his allies, but to seize London would be an act of war. He annexed London, but then handed it back to a new ruler of Mercia, Aethelred II, who was married to his daughter (and eldest child) Aethelflaed. Aethelred did not call himself a king, only 'Lord of Mercia'. This did not mean he was a mere viceroy of Alfred, but it did mean that West Mercia and Wessex now saw themselves as a united kingdom of the English. This was the key to the great achievements of Alfred's son, daughter and grandson in the coming years. Alfred died in 899, just before the end of the century, and was mourned by Anglo-Saxons everywhere.

44. Leather Working Was a Long, Smelly Process

Many essential items in Anglo-Saxon England were made from leather: shoes and boots, harnesses for animals and scabbards for soldiers, as well as domestic items such as cups, flasks, belts, bags and purses. First, hides were taken to the river to wash them and then they were folded and put in a warm environment, where gradually hair remnants and hair roots would rot, a process known as 'sweating'. To help things along, the inside would be soaked in urine. Next, the hide was 'scudded' or scraped with blunt-edged bones or blunt knives. To soften the hide it was immersed in chicken dung and dog turds! Once it was sufficiently flaccid the leather-worker needed to ensure it did not decompose any further by rubbing in animal brains, egg whites and fat, much like applying dubbin today. Another essential product the Anglo-Saxons harvested from the forest was oak bark. This contains tannic acid which helped to preserve the hides. Loads of oak bark were carted to tanneries where the hides were immersed in tanning pits, which contained water infused with oak-bark liquor. In Bewdley, Worcestershire, there is still an area called 'Bark Hill' where the consignments of bark from the Wyre Forest were unloaded. The hides were regularly moved and the progress of tannic acid penetration checked. The tanning process could take a year or more, a slow and tedious process, but one that had to be got right.

Everyone needed good stout footwear. Shoes were made by sewing leather with a waxed thread using awls or needles. Decorative designs could be incorporated by impressing leather with hot metal stamps. The leather was worked on an 'inside out' principle with the tough hair-bearing part of the hide on the inside. Then it was turned inside-out. The shoes were kept secure by means of a loop around the ankle which could be tied.

Actual finds of shoes remain extremely rare, of course. Leather was like plastic in our own times, ubiquitous and flexible in its uses. The army needed large quantities of ox-hides to make shield facings, a very tough and durable material. There is some evidence that the rank and file of the army, the *fyrd*, wore tough peaked leather caps for head protection in battle (helmets were rare, only for the warrior elite). Leather was soaked until it went soft and then stretched over a mould and heated until it became very rigid and hard. Scabbards were made of finely worked leather with elaborate designs. Clothing could also be made from leather, such as trousers and gaiters. Leather-working was a smelly, messy, labour-intensive task, but someone had to do it!

45. Love for a Nun Sparked a Civil War

Alfred had saved the day and had become the greatest of the Anglo-Saxon kings, so it was only natural that he recommended his son Edward to be his successor. Edward, known to history as 'the Elder' to differentiate him from Edward 'the Martyr' and Edward 'the Confessor', two later Anglo-Saxon kings, was the perfect man for the job. He had been put in command of the army seven years before and had intercepted and destroyed a Viking army at Farnham in Hampshire. The army was even more important in English national life than the Church and the kudos which came with military command gave Edward a crucial advantage. So, in 899 Edward became King of Wessex, and he had his eye on another title – 'King of England'. Unfortunately his succession was by no means straightforward. Edward had a rival, Aethelwold 'the Aetheling' (Aetheling means 'throne-worthy').

Remember how Alfred's nephews had been passed over in 871 so that an adult could become king? Now, the youngest of King Aethelred's sons, Aethelwold, was an adult, and in normal circumstances he could have expected to become king. Many Englishmen thought the same way and Aethelwold's claim to the throne was a solid one. Needless to say, the Danes in the five boroughs and Northumbria preferred him to Edward, who seems to have inherited his father's military skill and intelligence. Unsurprisingly Aethelwold became a very embittered and petulant young man, who felt cheated and betrayed. He decided to get married, for if he could produce a legitimate heir this would strengthen his already strong claim to the throne. According to the *Anglo-Saxon Chronicle* Aethelwold's choice of a bride was controversial. It is recorded that he seized a nun from a convent, disobeying her bishop's explicit ban on the match. Edward also proscribed the marriage and this caused Aethelwold to defy him. He took control of his own estates in Wimborne in East Dorset in a lacklustre rebellion. Edward was not going to let his cousin get away with this behaviour, and rapidly marched his army to Badbury Rings near Wimborne. Aethelwold swore an oath that he would 'live and die' there, near his father's resting place, but his situation was hopeless. He slipped away in the night with his illicit bride and sought sanctuary in Northumbria. This was a gift for the Danes, who immediately declared him to be the rightful king. He was putty in their hands and in 902 he invaded East Anglia with a Danish army and raided into Wessex. Edward immediately chased him out, but as Edward advanced he became bogged down in the Fens and issued an order to withdraw. Part of his army either didn't receive or disobeyed his orders, probably because they were intent on looting rich abbeys like Peterborough. This contingent of Edward's army was suddenly attacked by Aethelwold and his Danish ally Eric, the King of East Anglia, and overwhelmed, but the Kentish men put up a furious resistance. Eric and Aethelwold were both killed in the battle, even though their side won! Now there was no doubt who was the rightful King of Wessex – Edward the Elder.

46. A Warrior Queen Ruled Mercia

We have heard a lot about the Anglo-Saxon kings and their wars. Unfortunately these were violent times, and the people living in them were used to a militaristic society which idolised male warrior elites; it was a macho culture dominated by strong, brave, ruthless, sometimes brutal and callous men. Despite this, a woman, Lady Aethelflaed of Mercia, emerged as one of the most famous leaders of the time, and she did it completely on merit, against the odds in a male-dominated world. She was the eldest child of King Alfred the Great of Wessex, but her gender meant she was destined to look on as her younger brother, Edward, succeeded Alfred as king. Her mother Queen Ealhswith was Mercian and although she could never rule in her own right, royal daughters had their uses, especially by offering them as brides to the rulers of allied peoples. Aethelflaed was betrothed to Lord Aethelred of Mercia, Alfred's main ally against the Danes. The spirited young girl married her much older husband in 886, having eluded a Danish raiding party sent to capture her by hiding in an old fort. Alfred returned London to Aethelred as a wedding gift, and the two men must have been very happy with the deal. Maybe Aethelflaed wasn't so pleased with it! The couple had only one child, a girl, Aelfwynn, and perhaps due to a painful childbirth, or on account of distaste for intimacy with her husband, Aethelflaed refrained from sexual relations after the birth and never resumed them. Chroniclers at the time put this down to her purity and holiness, and maybe that was the reason.

The 'Lady of the Mercians', as she was now known, settled down to what she must have expected would be a dull routine at Gloucester, the West Mercian capital. But in 909 something happened which was to change her life for good. Lord Aethelred and King Edward of Wessex decided to launch a surprise attack on Lindsey, approximately where Lincolnshire and Humberside are today. This was a heavily settled, Danish-dominated area, adjoining Danish trading entrepots. For six weeks the West Saxons and Mercians burned and looted the area with the aim of hobbling the Viking kings of York and extending English influence in the north. Aethelred had another reason for invading. St Oswald of Northumbria's remains had been kept at Bardney Abbey in Lindsey, where King Aethelred of Mercia had interred them in the seventh century. Now his namesake, Lord Aethelred of Mercia, removed the saint's relics to a new church at Gloucester, St Peter's, which was the symbol of a resurrected Mercian power. Many of the Danes were Christians by now and this theft of the bones of one of the most powerful northern kings was a calculated insult. The next year two Viking kings of York, Eowils and Halfdan, attacked West Mercia in a mission of revenge. They penetrated as far as the River Avon, not far from Gloucester, then crossed the Severn and looted Shropshire. As they were returning home, laden down with booty, they were suddenly ambushed by Aethelred's army just east of Wolverhampton and the Danish army was virtually annihilated. It may be that West Saxon troops were sent to help Mercia, or maybe Edward himself reinforced them. Six months later Aethelred died, possibly of festering wounds from the dreadful battle. The time had come to make a choice. Mercia could submit to Edward and acknowledge him as King of Mercia too, or they could do something unusual, and select Aethelflaed as Lady of the Mercians. Unanimously they chose the latter course. Mercia was to be led by a woman, a warrior queen.

47. The Viking Invasions Stimulated the Growth of Towns

Gradually some towns had re-emerged, such as London, York, and the *wics* like Ipswich, but they were still small, few and far apart. The Viking invasions changed all this. They were experts at building strong and cleverly sited fortifications, which it was almost impossible to throw them out of. Alfred decided to build his own strong forts, called *burhs* and the idea was that one of these strongpoints would be available as a refuge for every rural community within a twenty-mile radius. Each of the *burhs* was also a depot, and had its own water supply and a large garrison. Edward and Aethelflaed had learned these lessons well, and now the brother and sister coordinated their assault on the Danes right across the waist of England, from East Anglia to Wales. Of course the Danes had their own forts, the 'five boroughs' and other major towns, but now, as Aethelflaed and Edward extended the programme of *burh* construction, new towns were established on the frontiers with the Danelaw. Some didn't make it, places like *Weardbyrig, Bremesbyrig,* or *Scergeat.* Others became successful and thriving communities which still flourish today, like Warwick, Bridgnorth, or Hertford. None of this would have happened had it not been for the relentless Danish assault.

Edward decided that the time had come to take the initiative and while his sister was busily building new forts in the west, he attacked East Anglia. He had been helped in this by a gift from his sister, who ceded London and Oxford to Wessex. These now became bases for forward operations against the Danes of the Midlands. A huge game of chess had begun.

48. THE LADY OF THE MERCIANS COWED THE VIKINGS

In the west Lady Aethelflaed had been busy. She was determined to deny the Danes the river crossing at Bridgnorth, which they had already occupied twice in her lifetime, and a new *burh* was constructed there. Others quickly followed: Warwick, Stafford, Tamworth, Eddisbury, *Weardbyrig, Scergeat,* Runcorn and Chirbury. In the north-west, on the Wirral peninsula, was a Norse colony, and of course the Northumbrian Danes had demonstrated their offensive power in the campaign of 910. Welsh malcontents murdered a Mercian abbot, Egbert, who was travelling with his companions in Brycheiniog, a small mountain kingdom in South Wales. Egbert was under the protection of Aethelflaed who was justifiably furious. Within three days she concentrated her army on the Welsh border and invaded the little kingdom, burning and ravaging as she went. Tewdr, the King of Brycheiniog, had no choice but to retreat to his fortified *Crannog*, a fort on a man-made island in Lake Llangorse. The indefatigable Mercian queen was not to be denied, however, and the place was stormed and burned and Tewdr's relatives taken as hostages, including his wife. The king escaped but when tempers had cooled he emerged and surrendered, promising to serve Aethelflaed faithfully, and paying hefty compensation.

This was a sign that the Lady of the Mercians was not to be meddled with, but could she replicate this success against the more serious enemy, the Vikings? In 917 she set out to show that she could do just that. She suddenly marched on Derby, one of the key Viking strongholds in England. We have seen how it was a tough prospect to storm a Viking fort, but this was achieved, despite very heavy casualties. Four of her most trusted *thegns* (the officers of the army) were killed in the battle to break down the gates. The loss of Derby was a terrific shock to the Danes. Viking myths told of how at *Ragnarok*, the Norse apocalypse, a warrior woman would emerge who would be invincible, at whose onset mighty warriors would cower. Next she besieged Leicester, which was the centre of a heavily settled Danish colony. She ravaged the country around the town so severely that it became clear she was irresistible. The Danes surrendered to her, and as a mark of her mercy, she processed into the town distributing alms to the poor. This clever strategy showed that she was prepared to compromise with the Danes if they would submit. By now, the noblemen and magnates of York, the Viking capital, could see which way the wind blew. A Viking pirate from Dublin, a pagan called Ragnall, had imposed himself as King of York. The Danes of York immediately saw the danger of prolonging the war, and also that Edward and Aethelflaed would never make peace with such a man. So, in the summer of 918 they sent emissaries promising to surrender to Aethelflaed. It was an incredible achievement, but a few weeks later, on 12 June 918 Aethelflaed suddenly died at Tamworth. Everything she had striven to achieve died with her. Her surviving daughter, Aelfwynn, was actually accepted as her heir, but she was only a young girl. Edward arrived in Tamworth and deposed her, sending her to virtual imprisonment in a convent at Shaftesbury in Dorset. She was the last ruler of an independent Mercia, and no more is heard of her. Yet Aetheflaed did leave another 'heir', her nephew, Athelstan, whom she fostered and brought up at Worcester. The statue of Lady Aethelflaed at Tamworth Castle depicts her with the young Athelstan, a boy who was to become one of the mightiest kings in Europe.

49. EDWARD THE ELDER BECAME THE FIRST KING OF ENGLAND

We have just about reached the half-way mark, and it is only now that we can speak about a king of a united England, Edward the Elder. By deposing Lady Aelfwynn at Tamworth, he had ensured that the Mercians had no choice but to accept him as their own king. Not everybody would have been happy about this, and there was an uprising in Chester against West Saxon rule. Edward offered the Mercian noblemen a compromise. His illegitimate son Athelstan was his favourite, and had been Alfred's favourite grandchild. He was an attractive boy, as William of Malmesbury, a later chronicler, recorded: 'He was of medium height, slender in body, his hair flaxen, beautifully mingled with golden threads.' Alfred had pampered him, presenting him with a purple cloak and miniature weapons when he was a toddler. But there was a problem. Athelstan, although he was the eldest son, was born out of wedlock, and Edward's legitimate son, Alfweard, was destined to succeed him as King of Wessex. Athelstan had been fostered by his aunt, Aethelflaed. Placed in the care of the priory school of Worcester, Athelstan probably spoke with the broad Mercian dialect and thought of Mercia as his home. Therefore, Edward may well have let on to the Mercian nobility and churchmen that when he died Mercia would pass to Athelstan to rule in his own right, while Alfweard ruled in Wessex.

By this arrangement Edward was able to consolidate his control over both English kingdoms, and he may have planned to incorporate the Danelaw too. Before he could do that, however, hard fighting lay ahead. The first immediate obstacle was to capture the remaining Danish forts of the five boroughs. Nottingham was besieged and surrendered towards the end of 918. Edward forced the Danish prisoners of war to build a new *burh* on the south bank of the Trent. He was magnanimous towards them once they had accomplished the task, and he ordered that the garrison of the town should henceforth comprise a mix of Englishmen and Danes. This began a process by which the Danes of the East Midlands came increasingly under English control. This deft political manoeuvring, backed up by a strong army, also meant that the Welsh rulers also acknowledged him as their overlord. Edward was dedicated to the task of making his new northern frontier secure, and he built new *burhs* at Thelwall on the River Mersey, Manchester and Bakewell in the Peak District. East Anglia was liberated and only the Viking stronghold of York continued to defy him. Eventually he was acknowledged as overlord by the Scottish king, Constantine. The Northumbrian Danes, although they were recalcitrant, had to accept the facts on the ground. England had become a reality. Edward died at Farndon-on-Dee on 17 July 924, the first king of a country we would recognise as 'England', but the Vikings were not finished yet!

50. ENGLAND FLOURISHED INTO A WEALTHY COUNTRY

One of the reasons why the Vikings were so attracted to the Anglo-Saxon kingdoms was because they were conspicuously prosperous. Offa's superior coins circulated all over Europe and they were noticed by the Vikings, who were very canny traders. Where did this wealth come from? Both gold and silver occur in the British Isles, but mostly in 'old hard' Britain, the mountains of the remote north and west. These areas were mainly under Celtic control. Most of the gold in the mines at Dolaucothi in Wales had been extracted by the ultra-efficient Romans. Silver occurs in England though, in Derbyshire (where there was also extensive lead mining), Devon, Gloucestershire and the Mendip Hills. At first the Anglo-Saxons had little use for coins except to melt them down to make jewellery. They imported coins for this purpose from the Byzantine Empire and Francia. They used Roman coins that had been ploughed up from their fields, thinking them to be 'fairy money' left there by elves and supernatural entities. But as soon as England had adopted Christianity and entered the civilised world again, coins soon caught on and the Anglo-Saxon kings could not get enough of them! Gold became increasingly rare though, and silver became the main precious metal used for Anglo-Saxon coins.

The quantities of silver in England were small. Most of the silver was imported from Germany's Harz Mountains. England was trading vast quantities of finished woollen goods like blankets and cloaks, which were of noted quality. This was the foundation of England's wealth from the earliest times. The coin supply was strictly regulated. After three years a coin had to be returned to the moneyer and exchanged for a new one. For every ten old ones he would give you eight new ones, a nice little earner for the king who controlled the mints. There were eventually over seventy mints located in the *burhs*, where they were heavily defended. Traders from abroad had to pay tolls to the king and these foreign coins were reworked into shiny new English ones! To discourage dishonest or corrupt moneyers there were strict laws and savage penalties for debased coinage, including having their hands chopped off and publicly displayed outside the mint! Millions of coins were produced and England became one of the richest countries in Europe. All well and good, you might think, but there was a downside. The Vikings realised that they could blackmail the English kings, who had absolute authority to order the collection of the *gafol* or *geld*, a land-tax imposed on the king's subjects, to bribe the Vikings to go away. It was a sort of protection racket on a massive scale, and usually it was worth paying up to avoid any more trouble.

51. THE CROWN WAS DISPUTED FOR OVER A YEAR

King Edward died in July 924, but it was not until September 925 that Athelstan succeeded him as King of England. Just as his father's succession had been disputed by Aethelwold the Aetheling, now Athelstan was challenged by his legitimate younger brother Alfweard. Alfweard had everything going for him and was immediately hailed as the new King of Wessex. Aelfleda, Edward's queen, was a powerful and wealthy woman in her own right and the principal churchmen of Wessex had probably already agreed that her sons should rule. A story was put about that Athelstan's mother had been a 'shepherdess' named Ecgwynn whom Edward had seduced, but this is very unlikely. The chronicler Layamon called her Edward's 'concubine', and it may well be that he was prevented from marrying her for political reasons. One consolation was that the Mercian nobles immediately selected him to become their own king, and from this power base Athelstan gathered his forces and awaited developments. Most of what we know about Athelstan comes from legends and sagas written about him after his death, by which time he was a superstar, a sort of Anglo-Saxon King Arthur. In fact, reading between the lines, it is very probable that Athelstan was cunning and ruthless, and that anyone who stood in the way of his ambitions would have been in serious danger. Alfweard died within a month of his father at Oxford, and was never even crowned. His younger brother Edwin was immediately proposed as his successor by the Wessex nobles but Athelstan was not to be denied. In September 925 he was crowned at Kingston upon Thames, the traditional venue for West Saxon coronations. He was anointed, a rite whereby the king was legitimised by God. His first acts as king were to grant estates to the Church at Canterbury, and to grant a slave called Eadhelm and his family manumission. Was this the sign of a guilty conscience? We can only surmise that Alfweard was murdered by Athelstan's agents. Edwin, his younger brother, was involved in an alleged plot against Athelstan, and died by drowning in the English Channel in 933, possibly on Athelstan's orders. This was the grim reality of the Anglo-Saxon 'game of thrones'!

This cruel and ruthless start to his reign has been largely 'swept under the carpet' because it detracts from Athelstan's subsequent glorious reputation. We should be careful not to besmirch Athelstan's character too much though. The stakes in medieval politics were very high indeed. Athelstan had to be defended by bodyguards even as he rode to the coronation – just as he probably plotted against his half-brothers, they were plotting against him. Athelstan was crowned not just as King of Wessex, but as King of England. This was a new power, one of the richest nations in Europe, and its enemies were gathering like wolves, hoping for a weak king. Athelstan was to be far from that, and his success in grasping the new kingdom tightly, against the odds, showed he was a tough customer who meant business.

52. Athelstan Became the 'Emperor of Britain'

The controversy and delay about who should become the new King of England was welcome news to the people of the Danelaw, Wales, Scotland and Cornwall. They all had much to fear from the powerful new state of England, which in the best scenario would exact crippling taxation from them, and in the worst case invade them and devastate their lands. The Danes of York had been dealt a series of crushing blows by Edward and Aethelflaed as we have seen, but they had not given up. Instead they had looked to the Viking kingdom of Dublin and its kings to ensure their continuing independence. By now the Vikings had begun to settle in the north-west; Norwegian Vikings had also established a kingdom of Dublin and the east coast of Ireland, and were still pagans. They already had a long-standing colony on the Wirral and even today genetic markers reveal a high proportion of people of Scandinavian descent there. These people settled in Westmorland and Cumbria, and in 919 the 'Clan Ivar', a kind of Viking mafia, took control of York. Sihtric, their king, was summoned to meet Athelstan at Tamworth, where a deal was made. Athelstan offered his sister, Eadgyth, in marriage to the King of York, on condition that he was baptised. Unfortunately Sihtric reneged on the arrangement, and died soon afterwards, leaving a young son, Anlaf, as his heir. Sihtric's brother Guthfrith immediately arrived from Dublin, ostensibly to protect the boy, but actually to stake his own claim. All deals were off. Athelstan invaded immediately with a gigantic army drawn from all over England. York was overwhelmed and its defences demolished. The city was looted but the churches were left intact.

Athelstan had coins minted at York, calling himself 'King of all Britain'. No southern English king had ever ruled in York before. Next Athelstan subdued the independent Anglo-Saxon kingdom of Bamburgh on the Scottish borders and in order to save themselves the other northern realms, Strathclyde, Cumbria, even King Constantine of Scotland, agreed to do homage to Athelstan as their overlord.

On 12 July 927 a ceremony took place at Eamont Bridge in Cumbria. All the lesser kings came to kneel before Athelstan and to acknowledge him as their lord, giving up their lands and titles. Athelstan then reinstated them on condition that they swore sacred oaths of allegiance to him, and he even ordered the baptism of Constantine's son to add a veneer of holiness to the proceedings. He also forced them to renounce all alliances with pagan kings, meaning the Vikings of Dublin. It seemed like a spectacular triumph for Athelstan, but the northerners knew he could not keep his army in the north for long. Quietly they were all seething with resentment, and as soon as he marched south to subdue his next target – the Welsh – the humiliated kings immediately started plotting against the so-called 'King of all Britain'.

53. THE GREATEST BATTLE IN ANGLO-SAXON HISTORY IS ALMOST FORGOTTEN

Athelstan's triumphal progress with his new English army took him to north Wales, where shortly after the summit at Eamont Bridge he winkled out rebellious Welsh insurgents in the mountains of Gwynedd under their king, Idwal Foel ('the bald'). Idwal was lucky that he didn't lose his head as well as his hair, and soon surrendered. As a result of his impudence, a crippling tribute was demanded from all five Welsh kings, even those who had not supported the rebellion. Cornwall rebelled too, but was crushed beneath the English juggernaut. Athelstan held a great court at the city of Exeter and, according to the chronicler William of Malmesbury, he expelled Cornish-speaking people from the city, rebuilding its defences. But Athelstan tried to be even-handed, and endowed churches there and founded the see of St German. Quite soon continental monarchs began to notice this imperial English power, and Athelstan married off his sisters to some of the most eminent rulers in Europe. It was not long though until Constantine, King of Scots revoked his agreement. The result was predictable. Athelstan gathered his army at Winchester and headed north. In ten days he was in Nottingham where another huge army joined him. Constantine had no choice but to surrender, and like Idwal he was forced to pay humiliating and crippling compensation.

The next year, five kings were forced to come to Cirencester, where they formally submitted to the 'emperor'. Constantine began to intrigue with the Viking Olaf, King of Dublin, despite his previous oaths. In the autumn of 937 a vast Viking army landed in the north, probably on the Wirral. Constantine came with his army to join them, along with his Welsh allies from Strathclyde. They fortified a hill called *Wendun* and awaited Athelstan's response. For a while nothing happened, but Athelstan was gathering the greatest English army ever known, so large that he had to divide his command with his young and dashing brother, Edmund 'the Magnificent'. The resulting battle was called *Brunanburh* and probably took place at Bromborough near Birkenhead, though this is still disputed. The English attacked in two divisions, Mercians against the Vikings, West Saxons against the Scots. All day the struggle went on, with horrific carnage on both sides, but at dusk what was left of the allied army fled. Constantine escaped somehow, and Olaf just about managed to get to his ship. The pitiful remnant of his army reached Dublin with only a fraction of his fleet. Constantine's son was dead, alongside five kings and seven Viking *jarls* or earls, including Owain, King of Cumbria. The *Anglo-Saxon Chronicle*, resorting to nationalist triumphalism, recorded how the thousands of Viking and Scottish corpses were left for the wolves and eagles to eat. For generations *Brunanburh* was simply called 'the Great Battle', according to the chronicler Aethelweard, but today it is scarcely known outside specialist academic circles.

54. An English Navy Patrolled the Seas

Alfred had initiated a project whereby Viking ships would be challenged before they even made landfall. New Anglo-Saxon ships were designed to be bigger and faster than the Viking longships and this tactic worked; as soon as the Vikings sighted Alfred's superior vessels they would withdraw and go to look for new landing beaches. It was a bold, ambitious idea, because the Vikings were instinctual and experienced sailors. This prototype Anglo-Saxon navy became a reality during Athelstan's reign. Before, the Vikings had always been able to strike in England and know that they would be free from retaliation. William of Malmesbury, the later chronicler who glorifies Athelstan, records that Athelstan assisted a Norwegian prince named Hakon by supplying him with English ships and troops so that he could reclaim his inheritance there. An English navy supported the English invasion of Scotland in 934, reaching as far north as Caithness. This was a sign of England's growing power, and was the thing that made other Christian European powers sit up and take notice. They were being harassed by the Vikings too, but few of them had taken on the pirates and won. They all looked to Athelstan as a new Charlemagne and to England for a successful, robust and wealthy model for running their own countries.

This was what had made the Norse and Celtic allies unite against Athelstan. They knew that as soon as England had control of the seas, they would be finished. As we have seen, they had united to overthrow Athelstan, but had been soundly beaten in 'the Great Battle'. Soon, even King Louis IV of France was begging for help from the English navy in his campaigns against his own secessionists. This was the glorious climax of the Anglo-Saxon Age, but it was to be short-lived. Athelstan died at Gloucester only two years after his glorious victory at *Brunanburh*. He was never married, probably due to some contract with his brother Edmund, so that yet another succession crisis could be prevented. He had been a great benefactor of the Church, a reformer of the law, a peerless war-leader and one of the greatest English kings.

55. England Became a Military State

England was born in bloodshed and war so it is scarcely surprising that its most hallowed institution was the army. The king only ruled by virtue of his (supposedly) hereditary heroism and genius in war, and his lords were military appointees, put in place to watch the peace, called ealdormen or earls (a term the English borrowed from the Danes). Every freeborn Englishman was expected to do his military service, and every community kept up a level of basic military training. Not every Englishman was in the army though. What usually happened was that the best trained and equipped would be sent as a representative, or those whose families had a strong military tradition. It was fearfully expensive to be a fighting man. Armour was extremely expensive, swords even more so, and both remained the preserve of an exclusive elite. Most ordinary soldiers possessed a spear or javelin, a lime-wood shield bound in ox-hide and a short stabbing knife. Rigid leather caps were worn, and for *thegns* helmets. Every man had a thick woollen cloak, and large armies usually rode to battle, but fought on foot, so a horse would be required. As the English became influenced by the Danes they adopted the Danish Great Axe, an axe with a foot-long blade on a five-foot helve which could cut a man in half and decapitate a horse.

Armies were not large by modern standards. The whole population of England was probably no more than two million people. At one of the largest and best known battles, Hastings, there were probably only between 10,000 and 12,000 men on either side.

56. A King Was Killed in a Brawl

It was no accident that Athelstan left no heirs. It must have been agreed with his two surviving legitimate half-brothers that he should pass the crown down to them in succession. Edmund 'the Magnificent' thus became Edmund I of England. All should have gone well, and at first all did. Edmund had fought at *Brunanburh* even though he was only about sixteen at the time, and was dearly loved, a sort of 'Prince Hal' of his day. He cannot have been more than nineteen when he came to the throne. The Vikings immediately saw their chance. Olaf Guthfrithson, King of Dublin, had survived the 'Great Battle' as we saw. For various reasons, mainly mercantile, but also because issues of custom and cultural particularism were at stake, the nobles and churchmen, including the eminent Archbishop Wulfstan of York, preferred Olaf to Edmund. York welcomed Olaf as their king, an act of open rebellion. Olaf took the offensive, marching into the five boroughs of the East Midlands. In the space of a few weeks, the gains of thirty years had been lost. Tamworth was taken by storm and a local landowner, Lady Wulfrun, after whom Wolverhampton is named, was taken as a hostage for ransom. The Vikings had returned to the former Danelaw.

Not everything was the same, however, because the anglicised Danish-descended folk of the five boroughs were now almost indistinguishable from their Anglo-Saxon neighbours. They were Christians who feared the pagan freebooters of the 'Clan Ivar', who seemed to them like Viking 'barbarians'! Many of them were relieved, therefore, when Edmund suddenly counterattacked, besieging Leicester. Olaf escaped alongside Wulfstan the treacherous archbishop but the

Viking army was pinned down. A truce was arranged, and a deal made recognising Olaf as King of York. This was a sort of Viking comeback but, fortunately for Edmund, Olaf was killed during a campaign ravaging Northumberland. Edmund showed his developing skills by his campaign of 944 when he deposed and killed Ragnall, the erstwhile King of York. Edmund invaded Strathclyde and blinded the captured princes of that country, intimidating even the King of Scotland into submission.

The *Anglo-Saxon Chronicle* relates what happened next:

This year (946) King Edmund died, on St Augustine's day. That was widely known how he ended his days; that Leof stabbed him at Pucklechurch.

Pucklechurch is in Gloucestershire and Edmund may have had estates near there, or was perhaps just visiting for the feast day. It is claimed that this Leof was an individual who had been banished some years earlier on the king's command, and that seeing him in his own presence the infuriated king attacked him, and was stabbed in the ensuing brawl. Other stories say that the king's steward was involved in a blood-feud, a duel to the death, with another man, and when Edmund saw his man was losing, interposed himself as the other man lunged and was stabbed in the belly.

57. Eric 'Blood-Axe' Lived Up to His Name

There are many revisionists about the Vikings these days, people who refuse to see the Vikings as many people have come to imagine them – bloodthirsty pagan marauders. Of course, there was much more to them that that, but somehow, I think their original reputation seems too convincing to all be made up, and I cite as evidence the character who is the hero of this fact, Eric 'Blood-Axe'. This man exemplifies all that the Viking era stood for; out of nowhere, he suddenly arrived to carve out a kingdom for himself and gain everlasting fame. His father had been the Norwegian King Harald 'Finehair' and Eric had succeeded to the throne of Norway, but then been swiftly deposed. Hakon, the young lad Athelstan had provided with ships, was Eric's half-brother, and was quickly accepted as an alternative to the wild and unpredictable, not to mention violent, Eric. There was nothing for it but ignominious exile in the windswept Orkneys, Hebrides and the Norse settlement on the Isle of Man, and Eric followed 'the whale's road' as the Vikings called the seaways, a true unreformed Viking to the core – pagan, even as the millennium began to loom. He was a freebooter, out with his crew for fame and fortune, his sword for hire and as soon as Edmund died, Archbishop Wulfstan (yes, him again!) formed a party inviting this unsavoury person to become their king! Suddenly the Norwegian adventurer with the gruesome nickname was in the big time. York was a wealthy and prospering trading centre, full of lucrative opportunities and important contacts. The people of York wanted to keep this to themselves as much as possible and reckless Eric seemed like just the man to keep the southerners out.

The new English king, Edred, Edmund's full-brother and half-brother to Athelstan, was not about to relinquish his control of a wealthy city like York, even to a hard man like Eric. England was still very powerful. Although Edmund left sons, they were mere children, so Edred was chosen. Within a year he invaded and ravaged the territory around York with such savagery that the nobles there submitted to him and abandoned Eric. Ripon and its mighty basilica was destroyed, the foundation of St Wilfred himself. Eric managed to destroy part of the English army though, before he fled into exile once more. In 952 Eric returned and was reinstalled at the 'King's Garth' or royal palace in York. He seems to have been involved in struggles on the Northumbrian frontiers for a couple of years but in 954 he was ambushed in the remote wilderness of Stainmore in the Pennines and killed. He was proof that the Viking spirit was far from dead and gone, and before long the Scandinavians were to make a remarkable comeback.

58. A Boy King Romped in a Threesome

King Edred died young. He was no older than thirty-three when he passed away in the West Country in 955. Edmund's eldest son, Edwy (sometimes called Edwig), succeeded him. He was a handsome, highly sexed young man, not yet fifteen, and was under the impression that a king could do what he wished. The English coronation ceremony was, and still is, a very sacred affair indeed. As soon as the complex ceremonial was completed there was an enormous feast at which the highest churchmen, nobles and foreign dignitaries would all have been honoured guests. The Abbot of Glastonbury, Dunstan, noticed Edwy sloping off from the feast quite early on. He stealthily followed the lad, and discovered him in a state of undress in a bedchamber, cavorting with his cousin, a young girl called Aelfgifu, and her mother, with the crown of England casually tossed aside! What a scoop it would have been for the Anglo-Saxon tabloids! Dunstan was absolutely outraged and bodily dragged the king out of the bed, forced him to dress, and returned him to the feasting hall. He severely admonished the lad and we know how teenagers react to being told off! Edwy became more and more wilful and disrespectful, always ready to listen to his girlfriend's advice. Aelfgifu hated Dunstan, and used her influence against him right from the start of Edwy's reign.

It had been intended that Edwy should only inherit the kingdom of Wessex, and that Mercia and Northumbria should pass to his younger brother, Edgar. Edwy's peccadillo, while of little consequence in itself, had ramifications politically. The relative calm in Mercia and Wessex had stimulated the growth of a new and more puritanical Church, influenced by the

Benedictine monastic order. Dunstan was a leading light in this movement, which sought to 'civilise' the English royalty and aristocracy, and to rein in their excesses. As soon as Edwy and Aelfgifu were married, Dunstan was banished into exile, probably because there was a question mark over whether marriage between cousins was legitimate. The purge did not just apply to the Church, but also to rivals at court, and powerful magnates. A great landowner, Athelstan, called 'Athelstan Half-King', had administered vast tracts of East Anglia and the Midlands ever since King Athelstan's time. He refused to continue in Edwy's service. When Edwy dispossessed his own grandmother of some of her titles and estates a movement emerged to depose Edwy and install Edgar as king. Seeing that the knives were out for him, Edwy rapidly backtracked and repudiated Aelfgifu, agreeing that the marriage was null and void. He was soon found a more respectable lady for his queen, but not long afterwards he died, aged only about nineteen. Was he perhaps a victim of yet another assassination? We don't know this for certain, but it could well have been the case. Edgar had already been accepted as king in his stead by the Mercians and Northumbrians, and civil war would have been likely if it had not been for Edwy's death.

59. THE MONASTIC MOVEMENT WAS REBORN

The man who had dared to chastise the king, Dunstan, was immediately recalled from exile when Edgar succeeded to the throne in 959, and made Archbishop of Canterbury. Dunstan was a moderniser and wanted to see a much more robust, sincere and well-organised Christianity. His model for this was the Benedictine monastic system which had been long-established on the Continent. For centuries, monasteries had more or less 'done their own thing' in England, and there were aspects of these houses which appalled Dunstan and his ilk. Some of them were 'double-houses' where monks and nuns lived in communities, and a mind which was given to prurience could easily construe scandal, even where none may have existed. Another issue was that local landowners were sometimes in the habit of gifting lands to the Church, and then appointing themselves as abbots or canons, which could be a nice little tax dodge. Dunstan was having none of this, and such people were ousted, to be replaced by celibate monks. Aethelwold, one of Dunstan's protégés, was made bishop of England's capital, Winchester, and he was very thorough in extirpating anyone who did not conform to his high moral ideals. He even took a female member of the royal family, Edith of Wilton, to task about her immodest apparel, and such attitudes did not go down well with many among the easy-going English, who found these intrusions irksome and offensive.

60. KING EDGAR HAD TWO CORONATIONS

Edgar had been crowned at Kingston on Thames like his ancestors, but the ceremony had been devised with another nation in mind – Wessex. The new king was not content with this; as he was now king of a united England, one of the most prosperous countries in Christendom, a larger, grander event was called for. First, however, Edgar had to assert his authority over the conquered areas so that everyone would truly accept him as their overlord. Cleverly, Edgar refrained from using military might. The people of the Danelaw were allowed to keep their own laws and customs and by this stage this was enough to keep them contented. Although many nobles were seething about perceived privileges of the Church, their opposition was muted. Edgar hired tough mercenaries from the Viking lands and Flemings to protect him as a personal bodyguard. In 973 Edgar was solemnly anointed and crowned as 'King of the English' at Bath in a ceremony that remains virtually unchanged to this day. But the King of the English was also overlord of Wales, Cornwall and Scotland, and his huge fleet of many hundreds of ships was capable of raiding Ireland or Europe. Bath was an old Roman city and the site was carefully chosen. Edgar, like Edwin of Northumbria in his day, was flaunting his (really rather spurious) 'Roman' connections, declaring himself to be what Athelstan had been in fact, an emperor. It was one thing to say this, quite another to enforce it, but Edgar lost no time in stamping his authority.

Anglo-Saxon politics worked on the same principles gang chapters operate today. A grand statement had been made and now a show of force was required to flush out any potential resistance. There was none.

How could there be? England and its king were just too powerful to meddle with. Edgar arrived at Chester to review his vast fleet and army. At least six minor kings came to submit to him, just as their ancestors had done to Athelstan. It is recorded that they were required to row him on a barge to his ship on the River Dee to indicate their status as under-kings. This symbolises the plight of the Viking and Celtic peoples as they lost control of the sea. Edgar's efficient civil service enforced strict *gelds* payable to the king to build the fleet. Now all the fierce nations on England's frontiers were Edgar's 'co-workers by land and sea', and instead of plundering England's wealth they were now forced to pay heavy tribute. Whereas in Athelstan's time they had formed a coalition, by now they were exhausted too, and were probably glad of a bit of 'peace and quiet' themselves.

61. A Royal Infatuation Began England's Decline

England was now at the pinnacle of its power, wealth and security, but in a little over a century it was to be overwhelmed, falling to a foreign conqueror. So where did it all go wrong? Anglo-Saxon society was male-dominated and misogynistic, especially following Dunstan's reforms. Women were either saints or sinners according to this perspective, and we should be wary of treating all that the chroniclers said as gospel truth. The chroniclers were almost invariably monks. Powerful women could be especially resented and vilified, and it was easy to smear them with salacious tales of how they had entrapped powerful men, especially kings. One victim of this calumniation may have been Elfrida, Edgar's second queen, who was to become the most controversial woman of her times. In medieval times women's sexuality was suspect, their seductiveness attributed to the schemes of the devil. Men, on the other hand, were permitted to partake in adultery and debauchery, and kings were usually allowed to take concubines as well as their legitimate wives. We have seen how Edwy had been admonished by Dunstan for his transgression at the coronation banquet. It is true that he was a callow youth at the time, but maybe some of this lust for the fair sex had passed down to Edgar too. The Church was doing well out of working with Edgar, and it was in its interests to promote an image of him as being a noble exemplar of all the virtues inherent in the West Saxon royal line, and to retrospectively attribute England's long national decline to Elfrida.

Edgar married young to a lady called Aethelflaeda, by whom he had his first son, Edward. For the first time in hundreds of years, the king had some leisure time, and any indiscretions were bound to be overlooked by the Church authorities. Edgar seems to have taken this as an opportunity to play the field. There was a rumour that he had abducted and seduced a nun (that old chestnut!) and found himself a regular concubine in the shape of Wulfthryth, who he may have attempted to marry. She gave Edgar a daughter before his eye fell on another woman, reputedly the most beautiful lady in England, Elfrida. The problem was that she was already married to Aethelwold, one of Edgar's most powerful nobles. A legend, which may be true, averred that Elfrida and Edgar hatched a plot to have Aethelwold killed while out hunting, a favourite method of 'bumping people off'. The story goes that Edgar was so besotted with her that he killed Aethelwold personally, but this is unlikely. Edgar ensured that at his second coronation in May 973, Elfrida would be crowned as Queen of England, something which had never happened before. She was now more powerful than any woman in all Anglo-Saxon history, and this may be one of the reasons she was vilified. But Edgar was blinded by his passion, and when she gave birth to a son, Edmund, who was indisputably legitimate, her position was enhanced considerably. Unfortunately Edmund died, but Elfrida produced another son, Ethelred, who she was determined should succeed to the throne. From that moment, England's decline was assured.

62. A Comet Foretold Desperate Times

Remember how the Anglo-Saxons were constantly observing portents and omens of disaster? The increasing influence of the Church had perhaps made them a little less superstitious, but Christianity was itself dominated by fears, and now, as the millennium approached, there was a widespread terror that the end was nigh, as had been prophesied in the Book of Revelations. It was anticipated that the Antichrist would appear in the year 1000 and that the Last Judgement would follow. In July 975 Edgar suddenly died at Winchester. It was a terrible blow, for despite his minor personal failings England had thrived and known peace for sixteen precious years. The *Anglo-Saxon Chronicle* eulogised Edgar, and when a comet was observed a few weeks after his death some thought it a sign from God of times of strife. Stars were supposed to have been fixed in their stations by God, and so comets (known as 'hairy stars') that appeared and disappeared and moved across the heavens, were attributed to the devil. The *Anglo-Saxon Chronicle* is explicit:

> Then too was seen, high in the heavens, the star on his station, that far and wide wise men call *cometa* by name. Widely was spread God's vengeance then throughout the land, and famine scoured the hills.

A terrible famine did strike England the following year, so severe that in coastal villages, whole communities joined hands and threw themselves from high cliffs into the sea. Famines were not unknown, of course, but now that the Danes had settled peaceably this disaster, along with the pestilence and violence that followed, were diagnosed as punishments from God for sin.

What made things much worse was that all the resentment and fury towards the Church that had been lurking among the dispossessed nobles was now unleashed in an orgy of violence towards churches and monasteries. Monks who had driven out the secular canons some years before were now driven out in turn and their estates ransacked. This meant great misery for the army of estate workers who depended upon the Church, especially following the devastating famine. The new king, Edward, Edgar's eldest son, was only sixteen years old. Despite doubts about his legitimacy in Anglo-Saxon society his age made him eligible for military command, something which ensured he was preferred to his legitimate half-brother, Ethelred, who was a minor of about seven. Edward was just old enough to be dangerous, but not old enough to be wise. He had a fearsome temper and was difficult to advise, even for the faithful and experienced Dunstan. Observing all this was the queen dowager, Elfrida, who may have encouraged disaffected nobles to back her son's claim, particularly those in the Midlands. Aelfhere, an ealdorman of Mercia, was secretly opposed to Edward, and all that was needed was an opportunity to strike. In 978 a conference was held at Calne in Wiltshire with delegates including Dunstan. The meeting seems to have taken place on an upper floor, and for reasons which are not entirely clear, the building collapsed. Dunstan survived because he had been sitting above a cross-beam, but many other high-ranking clergymen died. This could have been an accident, but it is entirely possible that some plot was involved.

63. An Anglo-Saxon King Was Finally Buried in 1984

The instability which focused around Edward's succession, and the potential rival to the throne, Ethelred, almost caused a civil war. Ealdorman Aelfhere had designs on territory in East Anglia, but the powerful nobleman Aethelwine gathered an army and defended the area. Aelfhere backed down; thwarted militarily, he resorted to plots that, according to legend, involved the queen dowager, Elfrida. Her chief asset was her young son, but with powerful protectors such as Dunstan, and ealdorman Bryhtnoth, who controlled Essex, Edward seemed safe. But then a rare opportunity came along. Edward had been out hunting, probably near Corfe in Dorset, when on a whim, he decided to stay over for the night at the manor in Corfe-gate where his half-brother was staying with Elfrida. Presumably messengers were sent ahead to alert the household to this unexpected royal visit. Elfrida decided to act, if the stories are true, and awaited Edward as he rode into the gate-house with a goblet of mulled wine or mead, as was traditional. Ostlers were waiting to attend to the king's horse, and as Edward stooped down to accept the goblet they suddenly grabbed hold of his bridle and stabbed him repeatedly in the stomach. Later traditions, possibly embellishments, state that Elfrida herself stabbed the king. Edward's horse was alarmed and bolted with the king still in the saddle but the wounds were fatal and he eventually bled to death. He was buried 'without royal honours' in a shallow grave at Wareham, according to the *Anglo-Saxon Chronicle*. The outcry about this regicide, the most serious crime an Anglo-Saxon could possibly imagine, was enormous, but Elfrida rode out the storm. She must surely have been aware of the plot, even if her young son, Ethelred, was in ignorance about it. Later tales told of how Ethelred had become hysterical when he heard of the assassination, and that Elfrida had thrashed him until he was quiet. The common people were simply stunned, and the *Anglo-Saxon Chronicle* summed up the national mood:

No worse deed than this was ever done by the English nation since they first sought the land of Britain. Men murdered him, but God hath magnified him. He was in life an earthly king he is now after death a heavenly saint.

Immediately, miracles began to be attributed to Edward 'the Martyr', and within a year his body was exhumed and reburied with high honours in Shaftesbury Abbey. Later, in 1001, Ethelred had it removed to an impressive new shrine. Ethelred became king, and now that her son was safely on the throne Elfrida's job was done. She was exonerated of any participation in the plot at the time, but this may well have been an exercise in damage limitation so that Ethelred's reputation was kept intact. Elfrida spent the rest of her life in Wherwell in Hampshire, one of the many nunneries and monasteries that she had generously endowed. Later commentators ascribed this to a guilty conscience. The cult of Edward's sainthood and martyrdom was international, and all his mortal failings were forgotten. During the Dissolution of the Monasteries Shaftesbury Abbey was devastated and Edward's grave was lost. In 1931, however, it was rediscovered and the bones kept in a bank vault in Woking until 1970 when tests on the remains confirmed them to be consistent with Edward's known injuries. For many years the holy relics were the subject of dispute between various Christian denominations. Finally, in September 1984 Edward was reburied hopefully for the last time at Brookwood near Woking.

64. A New Gentry Class Emerged

England in the tenth century was very unequal; indeed, the Anglo-Saxons would not have understood our modern concept of 'equality' and knew nothing about 'democracy'. Only a few men – the king, his earls and ealdormen and other high-born nobles – owned regions and vast estates. The Church was a great landowner, owning about a quarter of England's land surface. In itself the land had only limited value. The thing that generated income and wealth was the people on it, who were obliged by law to labour for the lords on certain days of the week or seasons of the year. It should be understood that the lords did no work as such. Their lives were spent in hunting and military training, and feasting. The peasantry existed to do the dirty work and to provide all the food, wine, ale and other comestibles for their leisure. What the lower orders got in return was security, or at least a promise of it. A new, intermediate class of landowners emerged who were granted small parcels of land on which they built farmhouses for themselves, with adjoining kitchen buildings and sometimes a small chapel or church. These farmsteads were sometimes surrounded with a stockade, more for prestige purposes than defence. In effect they were proto-manor houses of a yeomanry class, the *thegns*. One of the consequences of this was the proliferation of country churches. The surplus produce from the small estates increased because they were better managed and easier to oversee. This surplus could then be sold or traded for manufactured goods in the thriving market towns. Edgar had divided England into the shires we are familiar with today, each with its own county town. This new class of country yeomen were permanent fixtures.

65. The Clergy Reflected the Wider Class System

In late Anglo-Saxon times the Church interpenetrated all aspects of daily life. That one was a Christian, and therefore a member of the laity, was an unspoken assumption, and the whole community conformed to the expectation that the necessary observances and penances, and rites of baptism, marriage, extreme unction and so on would be performed. In very remote areas it is possible that some quasi-pagan practices survived, but these were rare exceptions. The higher clergy were very often from royal or noble families, and bishops were great landowners with large private resources, literally treasure chests of gold and jewels, such as St Wilfred, who divided his coffers just before his death. The rural clergy in particular were from a much lower social stratum. Educationally they were a mixed bunch, but many of them were virtually illiterate. It was expected that a clergyman should not marry but if he did, or kept a concubine, that he would at least be faithful to her exclusively. In theory, a clergyman had a higher social status, the equal of the country yeomanry, and so it was expected that their behaviour should be modest and seemly. They would withdraw themselves at feasts before the onset of drunkenness, for example, and they were expected to stay out of trouble with the secular law courts. Prayer books and service books had been growing smaller and were more portable, and over time the educational standards of the clergy improved somewhat. There were so many men ordained in holy orders in the tenth century that not all of them found adequate livings and were forced into becoming jugglers and entertainers, stewards and reeves or other trades.

66. King Ethelred Was Not 'Unready'

A few English kings have had sobriquets, like Alfred the Great, Edward the Confessor or Richard the Lionheart. But Ethelred 'the Unready' does not sound very promising! Few kings have been as vilified by posterity as Ethelred, but in what way precisely was he 'unready'? It is true that he was only ten years old when he came to the throne, and ealdorman Aelfhere and other leading nobles and churchmen ruled in his name until he came of age. This wasn't Ethelred's fault, and it probably wasn't his fault that his half-brother, King Edward, had been murdered. In this, as in so many other things, Ethelred was a hapless victim of circumstance, more 'unlucky' than 'unready'. Unfortunately Anglo-Saxon society judged its kings in the same way Napoleon judged his generals: 'Is he lucky?' If the answer was negative then the king was culpable, and his *fortuna* or luck being lacking, he was assumed to be out of favour with God. Ethelred was uniquely unfortunate, over a period of almost four decades. The controversy and outrage which followed his brother's murder focused upon him, despite his probable ignorance of the plot. His mother was widely denounced as a murderess and a witch, and in an unfortunate start to Christian life poor Ethelred had sullied the font when he was baptised (a notorious ill omen).

It is very possible that Ethelred was ill in some way. According to the chronicler William of Malmesbury, he spent long periods in his bed and struggled even to prop himself up on one elbow! He would then become so wretched and depressed that he would entirely withdraw himself, refusing to deal with the mounting and dangerous problems facing England. By all accounts he was a handsome and virile young man, and when he married he produced a dozen children by two different wives, one respect in which he did more than his duty!

Strictly speaking, 'unready' is a misnomer for him. His name, Ethelred, means 'noble counsel', but his long-suffering subjects made a clever pun on this, calling him *unraed* which means 'no counsel' or 'poor counsel'. The sense of this is that he would not accept good advice from people of honour and worth, but was always willing to take bad advice from grasping and malicious counsellors.

To compound these deficits in his character, Ethelred was a coward. This became increasingly evident as he came of age and ruled in his own right. Not everyone is a hero, of course, but Anglo-Saxon kings were supposed to have inherited the bravery of their glorious ancestors and this was one reason why they were born to the job. Otherwise it would have been much easier to just elect the biggest, toughest and most skilled soldier of the time as king. His tendency to shut himself away and ignore bad news, his distance from military command and his delegation of important decisions to sometimes incompetent and often corrupt lieutenants were all serious failings for any king. What made Ethelred's reign a disaster of the first magnitude was that it lasted so long (thirty-eight years in total) and that England's old enemies, the Danes, were gathering their strength and preparing to conquer the country once and for all. The most incredible aspect is that the English people, under vicious attack and unbearable privations, remained largely loyal to their unfortunate king, whether he was 'ready' or not.

67. The Vikings Returned but Bryhtnoth Stood Firm

In 981 seven Viking long-ships raided and burned Southampton, one of the busiest and most prosperous south coast ports. In the north the area around Chester was attacked. Next the 'sea-wolves' sailed to Cornwall, and raided unhindered in Dorset and Devon before London itself was targeted, and a great fire engulfed the city. These were terrors the English had almost forgotten, and they suspected, probably rightly, that the Danes had become emboldened because of the king's minority. In 983 Ethelred's regent, Aelfhere, died and the sixteen-year-old king took over, ruling in fact, not just in name. Here was a golden opportunity to rise to the new challenges but once again, Ethelred's bad luck was the spoiler. Especially within the Church there were eminent, venerable and wise counsellors on hand to guide the young king, people like the old holy man Dunstan, or Aethelwold, the bishop of Winchester, but one by one these 'old hands' died too. Dunstan was forewarned by angels, according to legend, three days before he expired, and like many leading English churchmen of this period soon became regarded as a saint. What was needed to counter the Viking threat was a soldier, someone of undoubted courage who would stand up to them. In 991 Olaf Tryggvason, a powerful Norwegian captain, sacked Ipswich, one of the most important ports on the east coast, but this time they were not going to have things all their own way.

It was not the king who marched his army to meet the Vikings in battle though. Instead an elderly ealdorman, Bryhtnoth, marched his own local yeomanry to oppose them. Bryhtnoth was 'old school', a giant of a man, resplendent in the finest armour and elite weaponry.

His job was to interdict the Vikings before they could do any more damage. In August 991 the English force drew up and faced a considerably larger force of Danes and Norwegians on the mudflats of Northey Island near Maldon. But the Vikings could not get to grips with them, because the English position could not be reached except by means of a narrow causeway only exposed at low tide. According to *The Battle of Maldon*, probably the most famous Anglo-Saxon battle poem, the invaders called over to Bryhtnoth, offering to go away if he offered them tribute of silver. Bryhtnoth was not the kind of man to give in to such impudent demands:

> We will give you spears for tribute! Point and blade shall bring us together first, grim battle-play before we pay tribute!

So the Vikings came on and stormed across the causeway. A terrible struggle ensued and the Vikings immediately went after Bryhtnoth, the bearded old warrior, and killed him. But the English fought on, grimly determined to avenge their leader. Byrhtwald, the ealdorman's deputy, encouraged the men:

> Thoughts shall be the harder, hearts the keener, courage the greater, as our strength lessens ... may he lament forever who thinks now to turn from this battle-play!

The remaining English force was almost wiped out, but they had made the Vikings pay a dear price. In all probability the poem was merely propaganda, but it recorded the passing of an age of Anglo-Saxon supremacy. The days of mighty warriors like Bryhtnoth were over.

68. The Archbishop of Canterbury Made a Big Mistake

Bryhtnoth's heroic sacrifice had redeemed some English honour at least, but the battle had been lost. Ethelred did try to act decisively, however. A fleet was gathered and a plan was put into operation to surprise the Vikings and burn their fleet. Unfortunately one of Ethelred's ealdormen, Aelfric, tipped off the Vikings who escaped with the loss of only one ship. Aelfric marched his men *away* from the enemy and Ethelred immediately suspected treachery. On this occasion, as on so many others, Ethelred was let down by his commander, and in the farcical aftermath of the campaign, he sulked. The debacle was observed by Sweyn Forkbeard, the King of Denmark, who correctly divined Ethelred's inherent weakness. In 994 Sweyn combined with Olaf Tryggvason in a fleet of ninety-four ships and attempted to capture London itself. The old Roman city walls were still doing their job, and after some weeks of harrying around the city the Vikings withdrew to find easier prey. The new Archbishop of Canterbury, Sigeric, had advised Ethelred to pay £10,000 in silver to Olaf to desist from his attacks after the fiasco at Maldon, the so-called 'Dane-geld'. Now, the Danes were ravaging in Essex, Kent, Sussex and Hampshire, devastating the countryside and slaughtering thousands. There was nothing for it but to offer another payment of 'Dane-geld', this time of £16,000 in silver. Ethelred was not the first or last English king to give in to blackmail. King Alfred had been forced to do it, and even William the Conqueror paid the Vikings to go away, but they did so to buy time so that they could raise new armies and return to the fight. Ethelred came to see the payments as a policy of first, not last resort, and by encouraging him, Sigeric had locked the English into a cycle of extortion and terrorism for many years to come.

The Vikings were not stupid. They soon assessed Ethelred to be a coward, and now, instead of high-risk enterprises where they would have to fight hard, bloody battles, like at Maldon, they could simply intimidate the English in large fleets and then encamp and wait for the efficient English government to collect their silver in the form of a land-tax to pay them off. These taxes were collected by the local ealdormen, and it may well be that they were involved in creaming off some of the monies for themselves. News was spreading all around Scandinavia and the Baltic about the weak English king and his fabulous wealth. New pirate adventurers soon set sail to make their fortune, and in 997 and 998 vast fleets descended on the south coast, burning, harrying and stealing as they willed. Individual English commanders tried to respond as Bryhtnoth had done, but with the same result. What was needed was a royal army, led by the king himself, but Ethelred vacillated and made excuses. As the dreaded millennium approached, the English people were paralysed, demoralised and convinced that God was visiting vengeance on them, especially for the sin of King Edward's foul murder.

69. The Wealthier Classes Became Increasingly Decadent

Just as in our own times people wanted to be conspicuous consumers to advertise their wealth and status. They became food faddists and animals began to be bred specifically for slaughter, veal and beef, suckling pigs, but less mutton and goat. Another craze was for fish. Herrings became an absolute must for any respectable table, and in truly vast quantities. For a really fancy feast the highlight would be a whole porpoise. Imagine the applause when the scullions carried that into the hall! All manner of freshwater fish were taken from the rivers or kept in 'stew' or storage ponds. A particular favourite was pike, as Chaucer tells us, but bream, carp and other edible coarse fish were kept too. We know this because fossilised human stools, known as coprolites, have been examined and analysed by archaeologists, revealing how diets changed over time. It isn't as grim as it sounds: they are no longer smelly! Also bones of animals thrown into refuse pits, or 'middens', contain remains from the feasts. More and more wine began to be imported too, and the wealthy began to display their prosperity by wearing fine clothes. Highly embroidered robes, hemmed with brockade of gold, even cloth-of-gold, were frequently worn, the colours bright and dazzling. England was full of expert female needleworkers, capable of the finest and most delicate workmanship. The Bayeux Tapestry is not a tapestry, but was embroidered by English ladies, perhaps ironically! Tunics and robes were not just more ornate and higher quality, but there was a lot more of them. Long robes seem to have indicated high social rank, and wealthy men wore rich jewellery and gilded ornaments such as brooches. For the very richest people, robes were made from silk, which had to be obtained via trade with the almost unimaginably distant orient.

This self-indulgence and display began to make the English aristocracy effete and corrupt, at least in some degree. They were also fiercely competitive and did not want to seem inferior to their neighbours. The new yeomanry class sought to emulate their social superiors and demand for luxurious imports and rare goods increased. The English royal court was no longer a rough and ready royal hall full of drunken warriors, but a sophisticated and tasteful palace full of colourful robes and dazzling vestments. Even before the Normans invaded, huge kitchens and bake-houses were built beside the royal residences (they had to be kept away from the main house because of the fire risk), and professional domestic staff were employed there to prepare lavish banquets, including the ultimate luxury, venison. For the poor peasants, however, nothing much changed, except that the demands made upon them to keep up this growth in consumption increased.

70. A New Norman Queen Came to England

The millennium came and went without the apocalypse and last judgement, somewhat to the surprise of some, but for those who clung to the eschatological perspective, the end time was deferred until the millennium of the ascension in 1033. Ethelred made a demonstration in 1000 itself and marched on Cumbria with the support of a fleet that shadowed his advance from the Irish Sea. This must have been an attempt to compel Scotland and Strathclyde to continue in their recognition of him as their overlord, but even this rather bizarre campaign failed to achieve its aims and the fleet had to content itself with a raid on Anglesey as it made its way back to home ports. It was a poor substitute for attacking the really dangerous enemy, the Danes who returned the next year in large numbers, raiding all along the south coast. The Hampshire *fyrd* confronted the Danes and killed many of them, but were defeated. The Isle of Wight, the key to the strategically vital Solent, was blockaded by the Vikings and so Ethelred paid yet another humiliating Dane-geld, this time of £24,000 in silver. It became clear to those nobles with any honour that this could not go on. Ironically the most aggrieved of them was a Dane, Pallig, who was Ethelred's own brother-in-law. He resigned and left the court, so exasperated was he at Ethelred's cowardice and incompetence. Other, more ambitious and devious men replaced him, such as Edric 'Streona' ('the grasping one').

All this was bad enough, but on top of this Ethelred's queen, Aelfgifu, had died. She had borne the king more than six children, possibly eight. This was sad of course, but it gave Ethelred an opportunity for a diplomatic alliance. His children needed a mother, and a very eligible lady was available: Emma, the sister of Richard, Duke of Normandy. The Normans were originally Vikings who had settled in northern France, a bit like the Danes in the Danelaw of England. They had become Christians, but had retained their martial traditions, and indeed perfected them, using the French innovation of cavalry. Their Viking cousins relied on Norman ports for shelter when they were raiding England and their wounded received medical treatment there. Stolen goods from England were traded through Norman ports into France. If Ethelred could make an ally of Normandy, not only would the Vikings lose all these advantages, but he would have the backing of a tough soldier with a powerful army in Duke Richard. So the marriage went ahead, and Emma of Normandy arrived to be crowned queen with a haughty retinue of Norman knights. She was to become one of the most extraordinary and influential women in English history.

71. England Was 'Ethnically Cleansed'

There can be no doubt that there was great hatred among the English towards the Danes. The Dane-geld, the constant rapine, pillaging and burning of towns, the terrorism and the famine were caused directly by their piracy. Yet still there were vast swathes of the Midlands and the north where a large proportion of the population were anglicised Danes. This was a perfect breeding ground for xenophobia. A newer phenomenon was the presence of small enclaves or ghettoes of Danes in large towns where they were engaged in crafts and trades. It is also probable that mercenary hirelings or bands of bodyguards for powerful men were settled as well, particularly along the frontiers of the Danelaw and in the ports, where of course there were also Danish sailors. Unable or unwilling as he was to fight the Danes, Ethelred decided to strike at these people, many of whom were respectable and wealthy citizens, and by now Christians. A secret decree was sent out to the tything deputies, shire reeves and military commanders ordering the synchronised liquidation of all Danes settled in England. It was not just a pogrom but a deliberate act of state policy authorised and directed by the king and his chief counsellors.

The day designated was St Brice's day, 13 November 1002. In Oxford the Danes were suddenly set upon by organised mobs and were clubbed and stabbed to death in the streets. Those that could ran for refuge in the church of St Frideswide, approximately where Christ Church is today. Some of them were armed, and they attempted to defend themselves but were burned out by the enraged townsfolk. Skeletons discovered near the location seem to be of soldiers who were stabbed to death and their bodies mutilated afterwards. We only have written testimony for this one attack because Ethelred made restitution to the town by having the church rebuilt, but he made no apologies for what he had done to the Danes, whom he called 'cockles among the wheat'. There were undoubtedly other similar massacres all over the country, and later chroniclers recorded traditions that it was widespread. In the Danelaw it must have been difficult or impossible to have operationalised the king's order, but whatever the numbers of dead, the real significance was that not even the higher-ranking Danes were spared. Ethelred's former counsellor Pallig was murdered but the most catastrophic victim was a woman, Gunhilde, sister of Sweyn Forkbeard, the notorious King of Denmark. Such a man was unlikely to leave the murder of his blood-kin unavenged, and set about gathering his fleet as soon as the news carried to him.

Perhaps 'ethnic cleansing' is a bit too strong a term for what happened. It was not a complete genocide, and probably the numbers killed were low, perhaps no more than a few thousand. But the intention behind it was exactly the same. To appease his bloodthirsty and miserable people, Ethelred had unleashed an act of state-sponsored terrorism. It was a cowardly, unmanly, wicked and shameful act which must have appalled any decent person, English or Danish. From now on the Danes would be more than mere pirates who would raid, burn, rape and go away. Sweyn swore an oath on the 'bragging-cup' to avenge his sister's death, destroy Ethelred and take England for himself.

72. Ethelred Became Widely Despised

The St Brice's Day Massacre, as it became known, was not just cruel and cowardly but also incredibly foolish. The anglicised Danish nobles of the Danelaw immediately switched their allegiance to Sweyn, whose fleet arrived soon afterwards. The Normans were dismayed by it too and their diplomatic relationship with England changed. Viking crews could refit in Norman ports again. Even Ethelred's Norman wife, Emma, may have turned against him. One of her Norman entourage, Hugh, had been put in charge of the garrison of Exeter. Sweyn's fleet arrived there, and somehow the city gates were opened to his army. The city was burned, and most of Wessex soon followed. Aelfric, one of Ethelred's commanders, confronted the Danish army but at the sight of them suddenly became ill and marched his army off without a fight. The countryside of Wessex was so mercilessly ravaged that there was nothing left to carry off, so the Danes sailed around the coast to East Anglia to try their luck there. The great city of Norwich was burned and sacked, and while Ethelred hid away in safety in London, the nobles had no choice but to bribe them yet again.

The Danish king seemed invulnerable, but he became too overconfident. He broke the truce that had been agreed and attacked Thetford, which also went up in flames, but while he was inland, a local ealdorman called Ulfkytel decided to scrape together a small local militia and oppose Sweyn, as Bryhtnoth had done at Maldon. His cunning plan was to delay the Vikings long enough for some of his men to burn Sweyn's fleet, which would have rendered him extremely exposed. Sweyn's army assaulted Ulfkytel's small force and were shocked to find that the Englishmen fought like lions. Eventually their numbers told, and Ulfkytel fell back after inflicting serious casualties. But the fleet was not attacked as had been arranged, so his valiant efforts (he was nicknamed 'the Valiant' afterwards) were ultimately wasted. However, this showed that the English could fight back, that the will was there, but they had no leadership from their king. As the years went by, more and more people, not just Danes but Normans and Englishmen too, began to distrust and blame the king, if not to actively despise him, at least in private. But no one could speak out, and Ethelred surrounded himself with sycophantic 'yes-men' like Edric Streona, a young *thegn* from Shropshire.

73. SWEYN GAVE WESSEX A NASTY CHRISTMAS SURPRISE

Remember how Guthrum had surprised Alfred at Chippenham at Christmas? Now Sweyn did the same thing. He suddenly marched his army by day and night, lit by beacons on the hills along the way. They reached Wallingford, fifty miles from the sea, and stormed the town's defences. To celebrate *yule*, Sweyn billeted himself in a church Ethelred had personally dedicated to his brother Edward. We may imagine how miserable this terrible Christmas was for the poor English peasants, but their hopes were raised when rumours of a long-awaited response from Ethelred himself began to circulate. The story was that a vast English army was being prepared, and was waiting to interdict the Vikings when they returned to their ships. The place where they would make their stand was the burial place of one of the old kings of Wessex, Cwichelm (remember him?), a mound called Cuchamsley Knob on the Ridgeway. The Danes were nervous because this was almost an identical situation to that at Thetford a few years before where they had experienced such hard fighting. But they need not have worried. Ethelred didn't turn up and there was no army, or if there was it was in the wrong place, far from any danger. Sweyn showed his utter contempt for the English by marching straight past Winchester, the English capital, with his entire army, loaded down with yuletide goodies.

Sweyn was paid an astronomical sum of £30,000 pounds in silver, nothing new there then! But alongside this there was a parallel plan. To get a grip on the collapse in morale a new archbishop, Alphege, was appointed, and he was a very sound choice: wise, holy and beloved by the common people. Also a fleet was built, hundreds of grand and expensive new warships. 24,000 coats of mail were ordered to equip a vast new English army. This enormous expense was paid for by an even more grinding land tax, but after two years of toil and sweat at last everything was ready. The next time the Danes came, the English were going to fight back, or at least that was the plan. Nothing could go wrong this time, could it?

74. THE ENGLISH NAVY SANK ITS OWN SHIPS

Now there came a fiasco to top them all. Streona had a brother, Beorhtric, who he managed to get appointed as one of the admirals of the new fleet. Streona really was a 'grasper'. He was paying court to Ethelred's young, pretty daughter in hopes of marrying into the royal family but his rank was too inferior, as yet. He probably hoped to infiltrate his brother into overall command of the fleet, and an allegation was made to the king by Beorhtric that another admiral, Wulfnoth, was a traitor. Ethelred was persuaded that this was true, and Wulfnoth flew into a rage and began to attack his own side using his own personal squadron of twenty ships. Beorhtric begged the king for permission to pursue Wulfnoth at sea and destroy his ships. Ethelred gave permission and eighty state-of-the-art warships were dispatched to bring Wulfnoth to justice. Maybe Beorhtric was too young and too inexperienced (Shropshire, his home, isn't exactly sailors' country) or maybe it was just plain bad luck, but the whole expedition was an unqualified disaster. There was a storm and the ships ran aground. Wulfnoth, seeing this, turned and burned the wrecks. Many inexperienced English soldiers and sailors drowned and all the hard work of two years was wasted. What few ships remained limped back to London for an urgent refit, but never played an important part in the war again.

The result was grimly predictable. Not just Danes but Poles, Letts and other Baltic privateers came in vast fleets of hundreds of ships to plunder the stricken country for everything it was worth. Fifteen English counties were ravaged by Sweyn's very mobile army (they controlled East Anglia, the famous horse-breeding area). Other bands of Vikings, thousands strong, devastated the south-east, and eventually Archbishop Alphege was besieged in Canterbury in 1011. He was betrayed by one of his own archdeacons and taken prisoner by the Vikings; a ransom of £3,000 in silver was demanded for him. He was one of the few good men left in a position of influence in England and the people were utterly bereft. What else was there left to go wrong? But worse was yet to come, again! Alphege, who had spent much of his life as a humble hermit living a simple life in solitude, rather liked being a prisoner! He refused demands for a ransom to be paid, saying that any monies gathered should be given out for the relief of the poor. He even set about preaching and making converts among the Vikings at their encampment at Greenwich on the Thames. This was something the brutal pirates hadn't bargained for but Alphege was pushing his luck among very dangerous men.

THE ANGLO-SAXONS IN 100 FACTS

75. A 'Wolf' Gave a Famous Sermon

The Vikings were becoming very disconsolate about the deadlock with Archbishop Alphege. He was stubborn and would not relent about the ransom. It signed his death warrant. The Vikings had intercepted a cargo of wine and prepared a gigantic feast. As soon as they were roaring drunk they dragged the old archbishop out and demanded he allow the ransom to be delivered but he would not, even when he was dragged to a post and tied up. Soon the drunken Vikings were pelting him with bones from the feast, until he fell unconscious. The cruel game continued until one of the Vikings struck him on the skull with an axe, some say to put him out of his misery. The murder was a new low for the English, and even many among the Vikings were appalled by it. His body was released for burial and rowed down the Thames to St Paul's Cathedral, where the solemn funeral took place. He soon became a saint, of course, with many miraculous cures attributed to his relics. Ethelred appointed a new Archbishop, Wulfstan, who was a stern moralist, but his next action stunned the entire nation. Ethelred hired the man who had abducted Alphege, a Viking pirate named Thurkill the Tall, along with forty shiploads of Vikings and took them into service in the English army, in particular as a garrison for London. Thurkill claimed he knew nothing of the murder and that he too was disgusted by it, promising his men would be baptised. This was the last straw for the English people, and at last someone spoke out, Wulfstan.

The prefix 'Wulf' occurs in a lot of Anglo-Saxon names: Wulfhere, Wulfnoth, Wulfric and so on. It means 'wolf' and Wulfstan used the pen name *Lupus* which means 'wolf' in Latin, a pun on his own name.

He wrote a sermon called *Sermo Lupi ad Anglos,* 'The Sermon of the Wolf to the English', that spelled out in minute detail what he thought had gone wrong in the country, pulling no punches. The sermon was read out all over the country for all to hear, including the king and Streona, if they were even listening. It was a trenchant critique of the collapse in the moral and social order since Edgar died. The law, said Wulfstan, had become ineffectual and corrupt. People were left to starve in destitution and sold into slavery. Vice and sexual perversion were rife, as well as drunkenness, black magic and witchcraft. Churches were ruined, monasteries defiled and ancient towns and villages burned to the ground. These sins were, he thought, generating a negative atmosphere which was feeding the Antichrist. That was why the Vikings had been sent – to punish the wretched English for their sins. There was only one way to get right with God. Everyone, the king and his nobles, even the wealthy yeomen, must fast and pray and do humbling penances. Wulfstan merely put into words what everyone was thinking. Ethelred had to go, but with his new bodyguard of elite Viking warriors behind the impregnable walls of London, it was hard to see how he could be deposed.

76. A Danish King Ruled England for Five Weeks

England was in meltdown, and Sweyn seized the moment. English lands north of the Danelaw had already submitted to him. Although he was a baptised Christian, Sweyn was no less a Viking warrior. He marched his army south and gave specific instructions that, once they were south of Watling Street, the old frontier, they were to show no mercy and give no quarter. Everything in their path was to be ruthlessly destroyed and even those who submitted to him as king were to offer up their children as hostages against treachery. Nothing could stand against this ferocious horde and within a few weeks nearly all southern England had capitulated. But Ethelred was still in London, and this was the key to the kingdom. Some traditions and Viking sagas state that Sweyn attempted to break into the city from the south by capturing Southwark. We simply don't know if the traditions are based on fact, but it is said that Sweyn failed, ironically because the Viking garrison of London under Thurkill's command destroyed London Bridge, then the only crossing. The old nursery rhyme 'London Bridge Is Falling Down' may be a distant recollection of this event. Nothing could save Ethelred now so he sent his queen, Emma, and his three children to Normandy where they found refuge with the duke. Ethelred remained for a while, but soon saw all was lost. He was no longer safe in London so he was taken to the Isle of Wight to spend a lonely and miserable Christmas. On Christmas day the English nobles offered the crown to Sweyn and so he became king, not that you would know that from the history books! It is true that he was never actually crowned, but that is hardly the point. The facts were clear enough. England had been conquered by the Danes.

So why was Sweyn's brief reign forgotten by history? It seems strange because these frantic events in 1013 and 1014 are some of the most dramatic in all English history. I am not alone in thinking this. In Elizabethan times an anonymous play was written called *Edmund Ironside* that depicted the power struggles after Ethelred's exile. It is very little known now, but some experts who have studied the play think it may have been written by William Shakespeare when he was a budding author. Sweyn returned to Gainsborough in Lincolnshire where his son, Cnut, was guarding the ships. He immediately sent out demands for more supplies and for payments of tribute, including from the shrine of St Edmund at Bury St Edmund's. Sweyn received a reply saying that the shrine was exempt from paying tribute under English law, which made him furious. What happened next is unclear, but we can easily see how the English may have embellished events to make a good story. In February 1014 as Sweyn was preparing to march on London to be crowned he suddenly collapsed and died at Candlemas. The English nation was overjoyed and attributed the miracle to St Edmund whose shrine Sweyn had threatened. The king was dead, and Cnut, Sweyn's second-eldest son, was very young and inexperienced. Thoughts turned to Ethelred, across the sea in Normandy. Could he, just possibly, have learned his lesson? The English nobles decided to write to him, inviting him to return only if 'he would govern them better than he did before', and promising that they would repudiate Sweyn's heirs if he would agree to their terms. Ethelred sent his young son by his second marriage, Edward, to meet the English nobles to test the water, and when he was reassured that it would be safe, he returned a few weeks before Easter 1014 to cheering crowds and a rapturous reception. Ethelred was back!

77. A Gallant Prince Rebelled Against His Father

Ethelred's original heir apparent, Athelstan, had died and so next in line was his warlike and inspiring son, Edmund, nicknamed 'Ironside'. He was nothing like his weak, uninspiring father and was itching to fight the Danes. There must have been many in England who couldn't wait for him to inherit the crown, but he had many enemies too. One of them was the new Earl of Mercia, Edric Streona, and another was Queen Emma, who now had two sons of her own with Ethelred: Edward and Alfred. Of course Cnut, who was still in England, claimed the throne as well. Despite all these potential claims and the bitter rivalries they engendered, Ethelred was still king (it does seem like a long time, doesn't it!) and for once the people were unanimously behind him. His sudden and unexpected popularity gave him the confidence he had lacked for so many years, and he raised an immense army. Ethelred's army reached Lindsey, where Cnut was encamped, and seeing that he was outnumbered the Dane set sail and left England with his fleet. Cnut was so enraged by this setback that he committed a terrible atrocity. Hundreds of prisoners and hostages taken by his father were mutilated, having their hands and noses chopped off. They were put ashore at Sandwich to terrorise the English, who he regarded as traitors to their oaths.

Ethelred was busy with some atrocities of his own. Lindsey, which had collaborated with the Danes, was thoroughly wasted. At last Ethelred could claim victory in battle, something that had always eluded him. He called a great council at Oxford to hammer out a new political settlement for the realm. Two of the delegates from the Danelaw, Sigferth and Morcar, were captured on their way to the conference and murdered at the instigation of the villainous Edric Streona. This was a return to the bad old days, and as his ageing father ailed, Edmund Ironside decided to act. The two murdered men had been his close allies. Sigferth's estates had been seized by Streona and his widow taken as a prisoner to a convent. She was a powerful lady of the Danelaw, an area which backed Edmund's claim to the throne, so Edmund immediately married her, despite Ethelred's objections. The king was now very ill and was bedridden near Portsmouth on the south coast when he heard the news that Edmund had raised an army and rebelled against him. Streona was authorised to oppose Edmund in the king's name, but Edmund was too popular. There was nothing Ethelred could do now, except what he had always done. He hid away behind the impregnable walls of London as his country fell apart again, but this time nothing could save him.

78. A Heroic King Liberated Wessex

Ethelred now did the best thing for the English people he had ever done, and died on St George's day 1016. It had been a long, hard reign, but he was still honoured with a splendid funeral at St Paul's in London, just before Cnut arrived with an army of 10,000 men to lay siege to the city. He surrounded London with deep ditches and dykes so that no supplies or people could get in or out. The nobles and churchmen of London declared Edmund to be the rightful king, Edmund II of England. The problem was that Edmund was busy gathering an army in the south-west, where Cnut had enforced his obligations on the nobles and received oaths of loyalty from them. As well as this, the Vikings who had defected to Ethelred under Thurkill had also joined Cnut, so in military terms the Danes were the stronger side. Thurkill was not the only defector. The wily Edric Streona had taken forty ships and joined Cnut too, so the odds were stacked against Edmund. But there was one thing Edmund did have going for him. He was an archetypal, 100 per cent genuine superhero. It seems very strange how a father like Ethelred could produce a son so radically different to him, but it does seem to be a pattern in history. People still told the old tales about Alfred's exploits as the saviour of England or 'England's darling' as Layamon, a poet, called him. Edmund seemed like a reincarnation of the great old kings of the glory days: strong, handsome, brave as a lion and unbeatable in personal combat. He was the personification of all England's hopes.

Cnut decided to use his advantage and strike before Edmund's army grew too strong. In a battle at Penselwood the two sides slugged it out all day in a bloody draw. Then, later that summer, a bitter two-day-long struggle was fought at Sherston near Malmesbury. Nothing could shake the English line, who were now inspired with a fanatical determination to destroy the Danes. Streona even resorted to hacking off the head of one of his own men who looked like Edmund, and holding it up shouting that Edmund was dead! The English were confused, but Edmund showed himself, and the English charged the Danes and broke them. The glory days were back!

79. Emma of Normandy Married Two Kings and Mothered Two Kings

Politics and religion were exclusively male preserves, which is why we hear so much about war and overlordship and power struggles between men in this age, but not a lot about women. There were some powerful and influential women, as we have seen, but they tended to operate behind the scenes, the 'power behind the throne'. The main task of queens was to ensure their sons' succession, as we saw in Elfrida's case. One woman stands out in this period because of her remarkable career on the English national stage – Emma, queen consort of England. She became queen in 1002. She was encouraged to take the English name of Aelfgifu, the name of Ethelred's former wife, which must have been galling to say the least. She was only seventeen and Ethelred was twice her age. She gave Ethelred two sons and a daughter. When Ethelred died it is unclear about precisely what happened. Both sides in the war were hostile to her children, Edmund because her sons were rivals and Cnut for the same reason. To keep her precious sons and daughter safe, she returned to her homeland of Normandy. As we will see, Cnut eventually became king, and in 1017 he offered a marriage alliance with Normandy. Emma was to return as queen consort, but this time to Cnut! It may seem to us an unusual arrangement, but it was a great success. Cnut was young and handsome, and although he was no saint he was an attentive and affectionate husband to her. She is the first queen in English history that we have a portrait of. She was nearly ten years older than her new husband, vastly experienced in the art of politics and had intelligent relations with key churchmen. She gave

Cnut a son, Harthacnut, whom she doted on and who she was determined should be king. We know from the *Anglo-Saxon Chronicle* that Edward in particular felt abandoned by his mother, possibly even betrayed. Her three previous children remained in Normandy, though she may have been wise to keep them out of Cnut's reach at first and perhaps this was the reason for this seeming cold-bloodedness.

A great drama could be written about Emma's long and exciting life, and she was a permanent fixture in English politics for fifty years. Not only did she marry two kings but two of her sons became kings – Harthacnut and eventually Edward. She was fiercely loyal to her beloved Harthacnut and when Cnut died she seized the royal estates and the royal treasury on his behalf. She also knew great tragedy in her life, as we will see later. She was involved in countless plots, intrigues and political crises and became a sort of 'national treasure'. She retained significant influence, so much so that she was accused of plots against her own son, Edward, but finally died in 1052.

80. Literacy Became More Widespread

Alfred the Great was literate, but he was exceptional, and hardly any king could read or write, much less the nobility. Three great catastrophes are responsible for the dearth of Anglo-Saxon written documents. The first was the protracted Viking invasions which destroyed nearly all literary evidence in the Danelaw and East Anglia. The second wave of destruction of Anglo-Saxon literature occurred after the Norman Conquest. The Normans abhorred and despised the English language and many Anglo-Saxon documents were burned or treated with such contempt that they deteriorated beyond repair. The last disaster was due to King Henry VIII and his Dissolution of the Monasteries in the sixteenth century, but there was one other threat to Anglo-Saxon documents which is often overlooked – fire. Even our finest piece of Anglo-Saxon literature, *Beowulf*, was almost consumed in a fire; in a society where nearly all buildings were constructed from timber this must have been a regular occurrence. Our main source for Anglo-Saxon history, the *Anglo-Saxon Chronicle*, was kept up as a continual record of major events, even after the Norman Conquest.

Important agreements and religious events were recorded in gospel books. Charters and wills were written down in Old English, as well as documents recording the freeing of slaves. Manumission of slaves was thought a particularly virtuous action and it was essential that these virtuous actions should be properly recorded, but also a slave might be challenged and retaken by the authorities elsewhere and an accusation made that they had escaped.

81. England Was Partitioned Again

We left Edmund, the new English king, as he was about to attempt the liberation of London in the summer of 1016. Cnut had suffered a major reverse and Edmund's reputation as the English national hero was at its zenith. He raised another army, the third in one year, and marched on London. We have seen how difficult it was to capture the city; Sweyn's putative attempt failed and later even William the Conqueror failed to take the city. Of course on this occasion the inhabitants were friendly to Edmund, but he needed to break through the Danish entrenchments outside the city to get in. Cnut expected Edmund to attack from the south and attempt to capture Southwark and London Bridge, but Edmund outsmarted him. Instead he managed to ford the Thames with his army and by a rapid march he emerged from woodland just north of the city at Tottenham. The Danes immediately panicked and retreated to Greenwich. They fought Edmund's forces at Brentford and were again soundly beaten, but in the pursuit many of Edmund's men, full of bravado, were drowned in the Thames. It was necessary to raise more men, and in Edmund's absence the Danes made another attempt to capture London, only to be thwarted again. When Edmund returned with fresh troops the Danes panicked and they were defeated at Otford, and at this point a familiar and sinister character re-emerged, our old friend Edric Streona.

Streona had switched his allegiance to Cnut, but he now offered to back Edmund with all his Mercian troops. He was a relative by marriage to Edmund (he was married to his sister) and was the most powerful earl in the land. On the other hand, he was notorious for his duplicity and treachery, and of course Edmund knew this. Much of what we know about Streona may derive from a lost saga which vilified him and blamed him for subsequent events, but they probably convey his character fairly accurately. Edmund agreed to take him back, 'than which no measure could have been more ill-advised' as the *Anglo-Saxon Chronicle* remarked. It was time for the decisive battle to decide who should rule England and the English were brimming with confidence. A mighty army was raised with three divisions: one West Saxon, another East Anglian and a third Mercian contingent. So crucial was the outcome of this battle that Edmund called for the bones of St Wendreda to be brought from Ely as a blessing on the combined English force. On St Luke's Day, 18 October 1016, the Battle of *Assandun* or Ashingdon was fought. The Danes had a strong position on high ground and the fighting to dislodge them was desperate and went on all day. The English probably had superior numbers and their morale was high, but at the crucial moment Edric Streona cried out that the Danes were too strong and retreated with his Mercians, leaving the other English troops to slug it out with the Danes. By nightfall there were piles of English corpses, many of them powerful English nobles, lying dead in the moonlight. Edmund escaped but the battle had been lost. Cnut lost no time in pursuing Edmund to where he was in hiding with a small force in the Forest of Dean. Edmund reportedly challenged Cnut to settle affairs by single combat, man to man, but this was the last gamble of a desperate man. Eventually the two men met at the Priory of St Mary at Deerhurst near Tewkesbury in Gloucestershire. Just as Alfred and Guthrum had once done, they agreed to divide England between them. Edmund was to retain Wessex, but Cnut would have Mercia and Northumbria.

82. A King Died on the Lavatory

The treaty at Deerhurst had specified that if either party died without heirs then their portion of England would pass to the survivor. Edmund now had two sons, possibly twins, but they were only babies. Considering the defeat at *Assandun* he had come away with a pretty good deal, but it was too good to be true. Within a few weeks Edmund, England's hero, was dead. On 30 November 1016, St Andrew's Day, he died, but the manner of his death is unclear. The obvious culprit in any murder plot was Cnut. Despite his later reputation for piety, Cnut was a Viking ruler, whose father's cruelty was legendary. He had mutilated hostages at Sandwich, as we have seen, but if he was responsible it would have been a disaster for his image among his English subjects. Regicide was a grave and heinous sin. But if Edmund was murdered, which seems very likely, there was another candidate, Edric Streona. He was known as 'an artful dissembler' and 'the refuse of mankind and shame of the English'. He had murdered Edmund's friends Sigferth and Morcar the year before, precipitating the civil war, and his treachery at *Assandun* had probably been prearranged with Cnut. He was deep in Cnut's debt, and a reasonable supposition is that Cnut, not wishing to sully his hands with the dirty business himself, put Streona up to the deed.

There are several legends about how Edmund died. He may have become the subject of some heroic saga which once existed, from which these legends derived. They may well have been based on actual facts, however. William of Malmesbury recorded that Edmund's prodigious strength and courage required the most devious methods to be used. Two young household servants were procured and infiltrated into

Edmund's household staff. When he retired from the feast to go to the lavatory (the only place where he was unguarded) one of the young men tipped off the other, who lurked beneath the privy in the ordure pit below. William of Malmesbury said that an iron hook was driven into Edmund's rear. Henry of Huntingdon, recording another version of the story, says it was done with a 'very sharp knife', but other embellishments even stated that some sort of crossbow was used to fire an arrow into Edmund's rectum, or that a spear had been thrust into him from beneath. All these stories have one common theme, the 'house of evacuation', and this tale seems credible. It was just the sort of assassination Streona specialised in, and even if he was acting on Cnut's orders, it was just the kind of dastardly deed we associate with him. It was a terrible end for a truly great king, who had come within an inch of defeating the Danes. A story goes that on Christmas Day 1016, Cnut argued with Streona while they were playing chess. Cnut, hearing of Streona's involvement in the plot to kill Edmund, had Edric executed on the spot. He had once promised Streona that he would 'set him higher than any man in England'. Cnut kept his word. He had Streona flayed alive, beheaded and the head stuck on a spike from the highest building in London. By this action Cnut was ostentatiously dissociating himself from the foul murder, something of vital importance to his public image, and may also have disposed of the only man who could prove his own collusion in the plot.

83. England Became Part of a Danish Empire

After two centuries of conflict, England had finally been conquered. With the vast resources of England at his disposal, it was only a matter of time before Cnut succeeded in establishing himself as King of Denmark. The English were now ground down by the most enormous Dane-geld ever levied on them. £72,000 in silver was demanded immediately and, in addition, £10,500 silver was exacted from the citizens of London. This was the price Cnut demanded for the evacuation of his fleet. Cnut kept a personal bodyguard of elite Danish *hus-carls* with him just in case the English proved fractious, but without leadership the English proved submissive. Edmund's sons were sent into exile, though the intention was that they should not survive. They seem to have ended up in Kiev in the Ukraine and at some point moved to Hungary. That they survived ensured that the line of Cerdic and Alfred was not extirpated. The same peasants who had backed Edmund attempted an insurrection against their lords whose object was to install Eadwig, Edmund's younger brother, as king, but the fight had gone out of the surviving English nobility and Cnut had Eadwig executed. Large estates were parcelled out to Cnut's *jarls* and to English collaborators. One of these English adherents, Godwin, son of Wulfnoth the admiral who had been responsible for the sinking of Ethelred's fleet, was given the earldom of Wessex, and was to prove the most important man in English politics for the next few decades.

When his brother Harald died, Cnut sailed with a fleet and an army consisting in large part of English troops to secure his homeland and eventually Norway submitted to his rule too. Sweden was invaded but Cnut was repulsed, despite valiant efforts by his English subordinates, including Earl Godwin. Cnut's original wife, Aelfgifu, 'of Northampton' as she was known, had given him two sons, the eldest of which, Harald, was originally destined to succeed him. Cnut's divorce of Aelfgifu had facilitated his political marriage alliance with Emma of Normandy, and her son by him, Harthacnut, therefore had a powerful claim to the succession. After such a long history of being ruled by their native kings, the English must have found the new regime oppressive and burdensome, but the strange thing is that this foreign occupation was not entirely resented. Now, a very curious thing seems to have happened. Cnut, far from being an alien despot, turned out to be a fairly good king.

84. Cnut Did Not Try to Turn Back the Tide

Cnut is remembered above all for the story of his being carried to the beach, where he commanded the tide not to turn, but this story is quite misunderstood. Many stories like this were told of the king, but this one has proven the most enduring. The earliest recorded version was by the chronicler Henry of Huntingdon in the twelfth century, where it is cited as an example of the king's 'great and magnificent' actions. Our conception of Cnut as an arrogant braggart with a megalomaniacal streak is probably the opposite of the moral of the tale. In fact, it tells quite another story, of the king's insight into the wiles of his flattering courtiers, and his humility and piety. This is what Henry actually said:

> When Cnut was at the height of his glory, he ordered his throne to be set on the sea-shore as the tide was rising, and said to the incoming sea: 'You are at my command, and the land where I sit is mine: there is none who dares resist my power. I therefore order you not to come upon my land, nor to presume to wet the limbs and clothes of your lord.' The tide, however, rose in its usual manner, and without reverence soaked the king's feet and legs. He, jumping back, then declared, 'Thus may all the inhabitants of the earth see how vain and worthless is the power of kings. Indeed, I am not worthy to bear the name of king before Him at whose behest heaven, earth and sea obey eternal laws.'

Cnut was said to have abandoned his crown from that day on, instead placing it on an image of Christ on the cross. So Cnut, contrary to popular belief, was portraying himself as a humble servant of Christ, even though he was one of the most powerful kings in all Europe. In fact, there are strong arguments to support the view that he was the greatest of all the kings of the Anglo-Saxon era, despite being a foreigner. In a great council at Oxford he agreed to reinstate the laws of King Edgar, the abandonment of which had been cited by Archbishop Wulfstan as the main cause of the disintegration of English national life. After forty years of turbulence and social and moral collapse, a strong man was in charge determined to protect the Church and promote justice. Another benefit was that with a Dane on the throne, the Viking attacks ceased, and for the first time in forty years there was peace in the land. Cnut was exactly the opposite of the notorious Ethelred – he carefully listened to advice, in particular from the learned and upright Wulfstan. Cnut had been raised as a Viking and had committed atrocities and eliminated rivals, as we have seen, but as soon as he became king he took the role very seriously. Perhaps there was a sense of personal guilt involved, along with a desire to atone for his previous sins. He famously attended the tomb of his old rival, Edmund, at Glastonbury Abbey, where he laid a cloak on the tomb, embroidered with peacocks, which symbolised resurrection. On the hill at *Assandun* where so many men had died, Englishmen and Danes, he consecrated a church, St Andrew's, to the memory of the fallen.

85. Cnut's Sons Were Notorious

Cnut was the most powerful King of England since Athelstan. Like his predecessor he invaded Scotland and compelled its king, Malcolm, to accept him as his overlord. Once his realms were secure he set off for Rome in 1027 on a pilgrimage with a large entourage. Emperor Conrad welcomed him with high honours and lavish gifts; a marriage alliance was even made between the emperor's son and Cnut's daughter Gunnhilde, along with gifts of large tracts of land along the border between Germany and Denmark. Cnut's mother was Polish and his influence there and in other Baltic lands facilitated a growing trade between England and that region. Emma's child by him, Harthacnut, had been sent to Denmark to learn the arts of kingship under the protection of Thurkill the Tall, now one of Cnut's most trusted men. Norway was becoming rebellious and a close eye had to be kept on the Norwegians, who threatened to break away from the imperial scheme. Harthacnut was being carefully prepared and groomed to succeed to the throne of England, and with his doting mother, Emma, guarding his interests, this seemed pretty much assured. But in 1035 Cnut, who may have been ill for some time, suddenly died. It was a disaster, because with Harthacnut out of the country, his half-brother, Harald 'Harefoot', immediately sought the backing of the English nobles, which he achieved. He was at least half-English, and the powerful earls of Mercia and Northumbria backed his claim. Emma immediately took charge of Cnut's personal Danish bodyguard, seized the royal treasury on behalf of her son and frantic messages were sent to him to return to England. Emma also disputed Harald's *bona fides* claiming that Aelfgifu, his mother, had been no more than a concubine of Cnut, and even that Cnut was not in fact Harald's father!

The man 'on the spot' was Harald, known as Harefoot because of his athletic prowess. He was crowned king before Harthacnut could set sail from Flanders and at this point Earl Godwin, who had previously backed Emma's son, switched his allegiance so as not to aggravate the new king. In the middle of this crisis Emma tried to get the support of her other sons in exile, Edward and Alfred. She still believed Godwin to be on her side, but she had been betrayed, and when Edward landed he was opposed near Southampton and forced to retreat. The other son, Alfred, was not so fortunate. He too believed Godwin was backing his mother, but when he landed in Kent Godwin had him arrested and sent to Harald, who blinded him and threw him into a dungeon where he starved to death. The broken-hearted Emma, thwarted for the time-being, was forced to flee to Bruges, where her surviving son Edward joined her. Emma was a very powerful woman indeed, with vast resources, and soon she and Harthacnut were ready to invade. Harald, however, suddenly died in 1040, and England was spared yet another bloody conflict. Unfortunately Harthacnut was a brutal, cruel and greedy oppressor. He always had one eye on affairs in Denmark, where war with Norway seemed imminent. His first act on becoming king was to exhume his half-brother's body and have it thrown into a bog! Things did not get any better. He increased the *gelds* to such exorbitant amounts that in Worcester two of his tax-collectors were lynched. Harthacnut responded by burning the city and wasting the shire, but the citizens had gone into hiding. Perhaps fortunately for the English, Harthacnut suddenly died in 1042, probably of an excess of drink at a wedding. He left no children, and so there was only one obvious heir available: Emma's surviving son Edward.

86. THE ENGLISH ROYAL DYNASTY WAS RESTORED

The centuries-long tradition of being ruled by the 'Cerdicings', as the West Saxon royal house was called, exerted a powerful emotional pull on the English. Even Ethelred had commanded unswerving loyalty until he was deposed and now, at long last, their exiled king in Normandy was free to return and the ancient line of kings was restored. But things were not so simple. Despite his faultless credentials and the immense goodwill towards him, Edward was only nominally English. He had been in exile on and off since 1013. Now almost thirty years later he was to return as king, mainly due to the renewed support of Earl Godwin, who furnished him with a magnificent ship. The price of this support was Edward's pardon for the incident involving his unfortunate brother, Alfred. On Easter Day 1043 Edward was crowned at Winchester, symbolising the resurrection not just of Christ, but of the Anglo-Saxon royal line. Unfortunately Edward's lengthy exile had left its mark on him. His mother was Norman and he had many Norman friends, particularly high-ranking churchmen. He had no experience of exercising royal authority, was unmarried and had a reputation for being exceptionally devout. England had been dominated by the Danes for so long that in large parts of the country, particularly the north, his authority was not whole-heartedly accepted. The main political player, Godwin, was the key to re-establishing control, and although Edward privately hated him, he also needed him. Yet although Edward relied on men like this to rule effectively at first, there was one area of national affairs where he was determined to have his own way, the great offices of the Church.

He appointed one of his close friends from Normandy, Robert of Jumièges, as Bishop of London.

87. THE GODWIN FAMILY BECAME TOO POWERFUL

Edward's lack of experience and his lack of important contacts left him extremely vulnerable. Perhaps the only person who could have guided him, his mother, had been alienated by him, and so he had little choice but to leave important matters of state in the hands of Earl Godwin. Edward was quite aware of this, seeking to counter it by importing Norman administrators and clerks. He distracted himself with commissioning a grand new church for London, Westminster Abbey, designed to be a showcase for the restored English regime, and many Norman workmen arrived to assist in the project. In 1051 Robert of Jumièges became Archbishop of Canterbury. Edward felt sufficiently established by now to resist the ambitions of the Godwin clan. Danish opposition to him had been contained or eliminated by expulsions of disaffected Danish nobles, and with his new Norman archbishop in control of the Church he felt confident enough to assert royal authority more vigorously. Godwin must have known what was in Edward's mind, and perhaps Edward's cool relationship with his queen, Edith, Godwin's daughter, was due to his desire to keep her in ignorance of his plans. Yet a confrontation with Godwin was a high-risk strategy. Not only was he immensely wealthy and powerful, lord of nearly all of southern England, but his numerous sons were powerful in their own right.

The most dangerous of them was the eldest son, Sweyn. His Viking name may have caused him to emulate the hell-raising behaviour of the Northmen and he was boastful, sudden, violent and headstrong. He openly claimed to be Cnut's son, not Godwin's, and ruled his own earldom of Gloucestershire and

Herefordshire as a mini-kingdom of his own, intervening in wars between Welsh kingdoms militarily. He seized Eadgifu, the Abbess of Leominster, and attempted to marry her against the explicit orders of the king. He had already been exiled once and on his return he had murdered his cousin Beorn in an unseemly brawl in the royal court itself. Godwin interceded with Edward on his behalf, but even he must have realised what a political liability his son was. When Edward began to settle Norman knights, such as Richard Fitz-Scrob and Osbern Pentecost on the Welsh border, and allowed them to build the first Norman castles in England there, Sweyn began to impugn the king's patriotism. Eventually Sweyn died whilst on a pilgrimage to the Holy Land, but Godwin's other sons were just as powerful, and all of them were given earldoms, so that eventually they controlled virtually the entire country. Harold, the next eldest, had been given East Anglia, and when Sweyn was exiled, got his old earldom too. He was shrewd and intelligent, but Tostig, the third son, was just as tempestuous as Sweyn. The two youngest boys, Gyrth and Leofwine, were also earls, and it was obvious that Godwin had designs on the throne itself for his family. If Edward was to keep them at bay, he needed to act decisively, and soon.

88. Earl Godwin Humiliated the Confessor

Edward's Norman friends now made their move. Godwin's ambitions were no secret and he had already attempted a coup against Edward which had failed. In September 1051 matters came to a head. Later Norman chroniclers claim that at around this time William, the new Duke of Normandy and Edward's cousin, visited him in England and was promised the English throne. This may be propaganda designed to legitimate the later Norman Conquest, but there was another foreign visitor, Count Eustace of Boulogne, Edward's brother-in-law. Eustace seems to have deliberately provoked an incident which led to Godwin's downfall. He and a large party of knights arrived at Dover where, wearing full armour, they intimidated innkeepers in the town demanding billets while they awaited their ship. When they were refused, an innkeeper was killed and the townspeople rioted and slaughtered nineteen of the Frenchmen. Eustace immediately returned to London and told Edward that they had been subjected to an unprovoked attack, which Edward believed. Godwin had authority over the area and the king ordered him to devastate Dover and the surrounding area, which was his duty, but Godwin refused to do it. This was an act of open insubordination and Edward used it as an excuse to banish Godwin and repudiate his marriage to Edith, probably with the intention of seeking a divorce. Edward issued a proclamation calling out the *fyrd* and Godwin had no choice but to flee into exile in Flanders, where his son Tostig was married to the daughter of Count Baldwin, his close ally.

At last Edward was truly King of England and he deprived Godwin's sons of their earldoms. But his new-found authority did not last long. The incident at Dover had turned public opinion in favour of Godwin, who portrayed himself as a patriot defending his countrymen against foreign interlopers. In the summer of 1052 Godwin, with Count Baldwin's backing, set sail with a fleet while Harold sailed with a separate fleet from Ireland where he been in temporary exile. The two fleets combined and entered the Thames estuary unopposed. The change in the public mood meant that on this occasion the chief nobles refused to back Edward and he was forced into a humiliating climbdown. Godwin was back, and now he was really in charge. Norman and French knights tried to flee England before Godwin and his sons gained control of the Channel ports but it was too late. Instead they rode north to seek refuge in Scotland. Edward was forced to take Edith back and seemed doomed to become a powerless puppet of the man he resented.

89. HAROLD GODWINSON BECAME A RISING STAR

The purge of the Normans included Edward's close friend and confidante Archbishop Robert. Godwin forced Edward to take Stigand, one of Godwin's friends, as the new Archbishop of Canterbury. This was a grave error by Godwin because the Pope backed Robert, and so the head of the universal Church was alienated. It began to look as if Edward's reign was destined to be as unfortunate as his father's, but in April 1053 Godwin suddenly died. Godwin had been a 'man on the make', a parvenu, but his son Harold was more genteel and accomplished than the rest of the family. He was handsome, intelligent, popular and a very skilled soldier and politician. Harold was determined to resist Norman claims, not only because they were a threat to him personally, but because this represented the popular consensus of opinion. Edward was still childless, and seems to have attempted a compromise.

There was one man whose claim to the English throne was indisputable: Edward 'the Exile', the son of Edmund Ironside. Bishop Ealdred of Worcester was sent on a mission to find him and bring him back to England, and in 1057 he arrived, only to die almost immediately, possibly murdered by agents of either William of Normandy or Harold. Harold must have been under least suspicion of involvement in his death because Edward now entrusted him with much more responsibility. Trouble had erupted on the Welsh border, where a powerful Welsh king, Gruffydd ap Llywelyn was attempting to unite the whole country. Edward was now well into middle age and had never been a military man, so he chose Harold to lead the army into Wales. In 1063 Harold made a surprise attack on Gwynedd, the most mountainous region, and devastated the entire country so ruthlessly that the Welsh murdered Gruffydd and sent his head to Harold, offering to surrender. Not only had Harold led a brilliant military campaign (he erected memorial stones all over Wales which were inscribed, 'Here Harold was victorious'), but he also took responsibility for the diplomatic settlement there afterwards. Two brothers, personally loyal to Harold, were set up as kings: Bleddyn ap Cynfyn in Gwynedd, and Rhiwallon in Powys. Harold could seemingly do no wrong and the ageing Edward began to increasingly trust him with affairs of state.

90. THE EARL OF WESSEX WAS SHIPWRECKED

Harold was now Earl of Wessex and the most powerful man in England after the king. What happened next is one of the most controversial events in English history. It seems that Harold either set out by ship from his estates at Bosham in Sussex or deliberately defied the king and went to Normandy to negotiate the release of two of his relatives who were held captive there by the deposed Archbishop Robert in retaliation for his removal from office. In fact the story of Harold's visit to Normandy in 1064 may be a later Norman fabrication, designed to discredit Harold. We will probably never know what actually happened, but the consensus of history suggests that Harold's ship was caught in a sudden storm and was wrecked off the coast of France, in the territory of one of William's allies, Count Guy of Ponthieu. Guy held Harold in prison for a time but immediately alerted William. Harold was handed over to the duke and the two allegedly became firm friends. William took Harold with him on a campaign against Breton rebels where he was responsible for an act of great heroism, rescuing two Norman knights who had become stranded in the quicksands off Mont St Michel. For this act of valour, William knighted Harold; but while it was the highest honour the duke could bestow, it also put Harold in a position of deference to William. The next twist in the story is also disputed and contentious, but according to the Norman chroniclers Harold was taken to the town of Bayeux where he was forced to swear an oath on holy relics that he would do all in his power to support William's claim to the throne. Some people say that Harold was tricked into this, but if he did make such a binding oath, it proved sufficient to secure his release.

He returned to England after his adventures, where (according to the Bayeux Tapestry) he was severely admonished by the king.

If there was an oath Harold would have repudiated it as soon as he was back in England, and it must have brought home trenchantly to him just how serious William was about his aspirations to rule England. The two men were now on a collision course, but Harold had problems nearer home. His brother Tostig was now Earl of Northumbria, where his outrageous behaviour and foreign 'southern' ways made him extremely unpopular. When Tostig murdered a nobleman, Cospatrick, the Northumbrian nobles rebelled and ousted Tostig. Technically this was rebellion against royal authority and the rebels showed they meant business, marching into Mercia where they secured the support of the new earl there, Edwin. Edwin's brother, Morcar, was selected by the rebels as their new earl, and the two brothers met Harold at Oxford and convinced him of the righteousness of their cause. Harold agreed that Tostig should be banished and confirmed Morcar as the new earl. He must have known that nothing could save his brother, and there was little love lost between them. This internecine strife was the very last thing Harold needed now. With William of Normandy and Harald Hardrada, King of Norway, both pressing their claims to the English throne it was absolutely essential to unite the whole nation in a common purpose. So Tostig fled to Flanders, determined to revenge himself on his traitorous brother. Events were spiralling out of control.

91. A SAINTLY KING FORESAW ENGLAND'S DOWNFALL

According to a *Vita* or biography of King Edward dictated after his death by his widowed queen, Edith, the rebellion in the north sapped the strength of the elderly king. He had by now become a sort of living saint known as Edward the Confessor. Pilgrims flocked to be cured of scrofula, a common disease which affected the lymphatic system, which Edward could allegedly cure by touching the victim. His celibacy was construed as yet more evidence of his holiness and his great new Romanesque church, Westminster Abbey, on which he had lavished so much treasure and attention, was nearing completion. In fact Edward did become a saint after his death. He began ailing in December 1065 and early in January 1066 he took to his deathbed. Great storms raged that winter and the whole nation was filled with anxious foreboding. Edward had a vision of two Benedictine monks he had known as a young man in Normandy, who warned him that within the year England would fall to the agents of the devil. He was said to have asked if there was any hope of redemption for his country, to which they replied that this could not come about until a green tree, stricken in two by lightning, came together again, and sprouted green leaves. These apocalyptic warnings were presumably disregarded as the ravings of a dying man, but for the anxious nobles and clergymen gathered in his bedchamber the real issue was who should rule after him? Edward allegedly nodded his assent when Harold was presented to him, and within hours of his death on 5 January 1066 Harold was proclaimed as king, despite having no royal blood whatsoever.

This unconventional decision was all the more unusual, because there was a candidate whose claim to the throne trumped Harold, Harald of Norway and William. This was the son of Edward the Exile, grandson of Edmund Ironside, called Edgar 'the Aetheling'. His credentials were impeccable. He was a member of the royal kin but unfortunately for him he was only fourteen years old, too young to command the army. It was clear that an epic struggle was about to ensue, and no one was in any doubt who should lead England and organise the defence of the realm – Harold. He immediately made an astute political move, and a great personal sacrifice. His lover, one of the most beautiful women in England, Edith 'Swan-Neck' was set aside, so that he could marry another Edith, the sister of Edwin and Morcar, whose backing the new king desperately needed. Harold II was, therefore, more like an elected dictator in a time of supreme national crisis than a conventional king, and that crisis could not be delayed for long. As soon as William heard the news his face turned black with rage and he resolved to invade England. As if to intensify the growing atmosphere of doom, in April a comet shone brightly for eight days, and many recalled the ominous precedent when Edgar had died …

92. The Normans Were the Most Skilled Soldiers in Europe

Harold had managed to provoke one of the most skilled and ruthless warriors in Europe, William, Duke of Normandy. He immediately sought the backing of the Pope for a crusade against England, which he secured. A few Norman knights had served as mercenaries on behalf of the papal authorities in southern Italy in 1017, and despite their numbers being tiny they had managed to take control of Sicily and Calabria. So what gave the Normans this military edge? They were Viking settlers, although the Viking element in the Norman population was probably an elite or aristocracy. The Normans were sufficiently assimilated by 1066 that they spoke a form of French, which although heavily inflected was recognisable. They were also devout, quite puritanical Roman Catholics. They had learned from the French the cult of the *chevalier* or knight, a heavily armed and mailed, mounted (the horses were often mailed too) and highly trained soldier, designed to smash through infantry, and harry retreating enemies when they broke formation. It was the blitzkrieg tactic of its time. The horses were trained to bite and kick, and they were specially bred in parks set aside for that specific purpose. The armoured knight, protected on one side by a long kite-shaped shield, would use a lance or javelin to stab down at his opponent below, then wheel around, and repeat the process. Horses were vulnerable, so more than one would be taken into battle. The sheer weight and velocity and noise of a large body of horsemen usually proved irresistible, and this was a new form of warfare, something the English had not yet perfected.

These parties of powerful knights were like small armies and, like the Romans before them, they knew how to erect invulnerable defensive positions, called castles. A steep hillock could be easily converted into a keep, the centre of a fortified base, with a high tower and an outer area called a bailey. Small garrisons of such elite troops could hold down vast areas and serve as a means of intimidating cowed populations by acts of depredation and terrorism. This was the nature of England's formidable enemy, and Harold was well aware of the high stakes, but suddenly his attention was demanded elsewhere – the north of England, and his enemy there was no less daunting. Harold had expected William's attack to come during the calm summer months so he ordered a huge English army to watch the coasts and the navy had been on constant patrols. The summer was dreary with rough weather, and William was pinned down in Norman harbours by the winds, contrary to his plans. By September it looked as if William would not be able to set sail as the equinoctial storms were coming, so Harold dismissed the *fyrd* in order that they could get the harvest home. Just afterwards news came to him that a huge Norwegian army under Harald Hardrada, the gigantic King of Norway, and his own brother, Tostig, had landed in the north.

93. King Harold Won a Stunning Victory

King Harold is remembered as one of history's great losers, but just a few weeks before the Battle of Hastings he won one of the greatest victories in English military history, a feat of arms which will never be forgotten by his countrymen. Hardrada and Tostig beached their ships at Riccall and immediately marched on York. Edwin and Morcar, the two earls of Mercia and Northumbria, gathered together a scratch force of 4,000 men and confronted Hardrada outside the city where they were soundly beaten. A system of beacons may have existed which conveyed the grim news to Harold in the south. He rode north immediately, riding day and night. When he reached Nottinghamshire large numbers of men joined him and incredibly reached Tadcaster in Yorkshire in only five days, where his 10,000-strong army took a desperately needed rest before pressing on in the morning. Hardrada and Tostig had ridden out to a small bridge over the Derwent called Stamford Bridge on 25 September to receive hostages and supplies they had been promised by the citizens of York. He had about half his army with him, having left the rest at Riccall, and because it was a hot day, none of them had their chainmail shirts on. As they were sunbathing they suddenly noticed the glimmer of sunlight on thousands of chainmail coats and weapons, and a dust-cloud caused by thousands of horses. Harold had arrived.

Hardrada selected his biggest, toughest man, and tasked him with defending the bridge on his own with a Danish great-axe. He managed to kill forty men before he was speared by a man from underneath the bridge in a boat. The English rushed over the bridge and smashed into the Viking shield wall. Looking for Hardrada beneath the banners, the English easily picked him out due to his exceptional height (well over six feet) and targeted him with arrows. He fell with an arrow through his throat but Tostig, defying his hated brother, picked up the banner and carried on the fight. It was a hopeless position for the Vikings but suddenly their comrades from Riccall, alerted by a messenger Hardrada had sent, arrived, having run nearly twenty miles. They smashed into the English and began to beat them back, but Harold, realising how exhausted they were, led a counter-attack. The spent Norwegians were forced into a death-circle and slaughtered almost to the last man. Their bones were formed into a cairn there which was still visible a century later. Tostig lay dead, and only a few Viking ships were allowed to return home. Harold took vast booty including gold bullion from the Viking encampment. The Battle of Stamford Bridge was an incredible victory against the toughest warrior in Europe but Harold did not have much time to enjoy his glory. He was still at his victory feast in York when news came from the south. It was bad. William and his army had landed at Pevensey Bay in Sussex. Harold had to turn his army around and take his troops all the way back to fight another grim battle.

94. A Surprise Attack Was Foiled

Harold had personal estates in Sussex and William knew this. The Normans immediately began to burn all the villages and to terrorise the inhabitants around their encampment. This was designed to provoke Harold into precipitate action but, as we have seen, Harold believed in swift, surprise attacks anyway. He left York immediately with his own personal troops, but perhaps he made a mistake at this point. He had neglected to share out the booty from Hardrada's camp, and many of the specialist Danish mercenaries may have resented this and not taken service for the next battle. But Harold's mind was on William, and he resolved to go out to meet him in battle as soon as possible. The casualties at Stamford Bridge had been heavy, so Harold needed to gather a new army. When he reached London he sent out word to all the men of the southern shires to send their forces. After four days' rest Harold marched out of London; he had arranged to meet the rest of the English army at 'the hoar-apple tree' on Caldbec Hill, just off the London–Hastings road. Harold left on 12 October and on the evening of the 13th English scouts ran into Norman pickets. Harold had wanted to attack the Normans before they were ready at dawn, but now this plan was foiled. William was alerted and roused his troops. By 6 a.m. his forces were on the move. It was still dark and in the confusion William had put his chainmail coat on back-to-front! Unfortunately this was considered bad luck, but William made light of the incident. As soon as the sun was up William studied the English position. It was extremely strong. A ridge, 1,000 yards long, was flanked on either side by boggy ground, impassable to horses. On top of the steep ridge Harold had placed his banners and 12,000 men, twelve ranks deep, stood in a solid shield wall atop it. In the front ranks waited the Danish great-axe men who could cut off a horse's head with a single blow. It was going to be a long day.

William had at least 10,000 men. He divided his army into three sections. On his left flank were his Breton allies, equipped in a similar fashion to the Normans; in the centre were his elite Norman knights and men-at-arms; and on his right flank were the French and Flemish mercenaries. In a screen to his front a body of archers, some of them Genoese crossbowmen, unleashed their volleys at the English line. William mounted his Spanish *destrier* or armoured war-horse, and reviewed his troops, when just before 9 a.m. a Norman knight, Taillefer, rode into the English line, juggling his mace and taunting them. He was rapidly killed, and immediately the Battle of Hastings commenced.

95. THE BATTLE OF HASTINGS WAS NOT IN HASTINGS

William's first attack was a general attack on the entire English front line. The English army had taken most of the enemy arrows on their shields, and as soon as the Norman army came within range the English unleashed the 'battle-shower', a discharge of thousands of rocks, hatchets, clubs, javelins and other missiles. The Normans recoiled and as soon as their infantry closed with the English front rank the axe-men emerged and did grievous damage. The Bretons on William's left flank broke and ran, and the English, wild with sudden enthusiasm, ran after them down the slope. William, seeing his chance, launched an all-out attack on the men who had broken ranks. They ran to a small hillock where they formed up, but were ruthlessly wiped out in a matter of a few minutes. This was a disaster for Harold, whose brothers, Gyrth and Leofwine, had been killed in the first attack. Both sides reformed and took stock. William may well have given orders to provoke the English by feigned retreats, because the next attack was more coordinated. The archers moved in closer and their volleys preceded each Norman charge. The English were still resisting manfully, however, and the French and Flemish troops took a severe mauling. William had already lost two horses when suddenly he went down again, and a rumour spread that he was dead. William struggled onto yet another mount, and removed his helmet so that his men could see he was alive, and shouted to them that God would still give them victory. The Normans returned to the attack and the English line began to visibly buckle. Archers targeted the banners where Harold and his bodyguard were gathered, and

Harold was struck in the eye with an arrow. Four Norman knights hacked their way through to him, and he was speared through, beheaded, disembowelled and his genitals hacked off. As the news spread, the rear ranks began to run to the woods in the dusk of early evening, but Harold's elite bodyguard remained by his mangled corpse until they too were all killed. As the Normans pursued the retreating Englishmen their horses stumbled into a hidden ravine, called 'malfosse', and the English returned to slit their throats.

William received a visitor later that evening. It was Edith 'Swan-Neck', Harold's lover, who had come to plead for his body. She could only recognise it because of 'certain intimate marks' which only she knew. Harold's remains were taken away, perhaps to be buried at his family estates near Bosham nearby, or at Waltham Abbey which he had endowed. Some legends say he did not die, but had survived, living as a hermit in Chester until he died at a great age. But Harold, the last Anglo-Saxon king, was dead. However, the Anglo-Saxons were not finished yet, and William was not yet crowned king. One battle was not the whole war, but we should not underestimate what a catastrophe it was for England. Perhaps as many as 5,000 Englishmen were killed in the battle, and William marked the spot where Harold fell by building an abbey, Battle Abbey. The village of Battle in East Sussex is the actual battlefield, about eight miles north of Hastings, but the battle is generally known by the name of that nearby town.

96. London Burned as William Was Crowned

The Anglo-Saxons (and Anglo-Danes) were ready to submit. Edgar the Aetheling was still alive and, as we have seen, there was no dispute about his royal credentials. But he was only a boy, against a man – and what a man! William was not going to give up his claim to anyone, and the English army had been practically destroyed. His problem was London. His army had probably lost a third of its strength and many horses too, and to make matters worse there was an outbreak of dysentery in his camp as winter came on. He tried to assault London from Southwark over London Bridge but was repulsed. In revenge he burned Southwark and then rode around the city, devastating all villages in his path. It was obvious that he wasn't going anywhere, and when Harold's widow surrendered the royal treasury to William, many leading men decided to capitulate.

Archbishop Ealdred of York and Edgar the Aetheling, along with the earls of Mercia and Northumbria Edwin and Morcar, rode out to William and surrendered at Berkhamsted. On Christmas Day 1066, England saw its third ruler in one year crowned as king. William trembled as the crown was placed on his head and he was asked to take the most sacred oath to rule with justice over all. The Anglo-Saxon nobles in Westminster Abbey shouted out their assent, but Norman guards outside were terrified and thought a rebellion had broken out. They charged the crowds of peaceful onlookers, killing many, and several buildings were set alight.

William's reign had got off to a shaky start and there was much more drama to come, but at first things went fairly smoothly. One of the reasons why the

English had surrendered was because of the power vacuum created by so many of the nobles of the south perishing at Hastings; William lost no time in giving out these vacant estates to his best friends and most faithful supporters, including members of his family. The English nobles thought that the surviving *thegn* class, those who had not supported Harold, would be left alone, and the chief churchmen thought they were safe too. In fact William intended no such thing.

After a while William felt secure enough to return to his homeland to see his queen, Matilda, leaving England in the charge of two men he trusted implicitly: Odo, his half-brother, in the south, and William Fitz-Osbern in the north. At this time a huge number of Norman castles were built all over the country, using English forced labour. These were quite simple but very effective timber constructions, not the huge stone structures which came later on. Major towns were forced into demolishing areas of dense occupation to make way for the garrisons of arrogant, brutal Norman and 'French' (the English called them all 'French') troops. By the time William returned a rebellion had taken place at Exeter, encouraged by Harold's mother and his illegitimate sons. William gathered an army of composite Norman and English troops and laid siege to the city, which defied him for eighteen days before surrendering. William was quite merciful (he had once chopped off the hands and feet of the inhabitants of a town which had rebelled against him) but it was not only in the south-west where trouble was brewing. On the Welsh border, in the Midlands, in Yorkshire and the north – basically everywhere where his occupying forces were weak – rebellion and insurrection was in the air.

97. WILLIAM 'THE BASTARD' COMMITTED A CRIME AGAINST HUMANITY

The Normans treated the conquered English with contempt and a backlash soon came. Ironically it was in the area where there had been a Norman presence longest, the Welsh border counties of Herefordshire and Shropshire, where they were first attacked. Remember Edric Streona? Now, a relation of his, also called Edric 'the Wild', had rebelled against the king, slaughtered Norman men-at-arms in the wildernesses of Clun Forest and finally had allied himself with Bleddyn of Gwynedd and Rhiwallon of Powys, the two brothers who had been liege men of Harold. They laid siege to Hereford and plundered the entire area before they withdrew, where Edric 'the Forester', as he is sometimes known, waged a guerrilla war from the dense woodlands and steep hills. But there was bigger trouble brewing in the north. Edgar the Aetheling was now in exile in Scotland, and the King of Scots, Malcolm, hoped to use him by supporting rebellions against William in the north of England. Meanwhile, the nobility and churchmen of York and Durham were hatching schemes of their own. Their plan was the one we have seen many times before – to call in the Vikings as liberators. King Sweyn of Denmark (Sweyn Estrithson) gathered a fleet of 240 ships full of pirates from all over the Baltic, and landed in the Humber estuary. At about the same time, Harold's sons raided in the south-west with a fleet from Ireland. When William marched north to deal with this threat, simultaneous risings took place in Staffordshire, Shropshire and the south-west. William seized York, and seems to have paid the Vikings to stay quiet. The king's mood was grim, and he now resolved on a policy which can only be described as a war-crime.

It is not usually a good idea to apply our modern standards to history, but this judgement was made by chroniclers at the time, like the Shropshire writer Orderic Vitalis. What William did was to order his army to devastate the whole of Yorkshire and Durham in the middle of winter. All villages and towns were burned, all ploughs destroyed and all livestock slaughtered. No one was safe, and over 100,000 people perished. The famine was so severe that people ate the dead bodies of their relatives. Those who survived had no seed-corn and slowly died of starvation or sold themselves into slavery across the border. This was one of the most monstrous acts in medieval history, but it achieved its aim. William marched south and his reputation went before him. One by one the rebellions fizzled out, and huge new castles were constructed in areas of disaffection. William had taken an iron grip of the country, but even now, when all seemed lost, the English continued a desperate outlaw resistance.

98. The Last Anglo-Saxon Heroes Were Prototypes for Robin Hood

The rebellion of 1069 had failed. Now William was free to persecute, exclude and demean the English people. The Church in particular was purged of Englishmen. News of the horrors in the north reached the ear of the Pope. Only one Anglo-Saxon bishop remained by 1075; bishops had been prime-movers in the northern rebellion. Huge tracts of England were given to a select few Norman nobles, and of course virtually all Church land was in Norman hands. Because they were so few, only tens of thousands at first, the Normans extended a law called *murdrum* in case any of them were ambushed, which obliged the neighbourhood to give up the offender or face crippling fines. From the castles the Normans launched forays to raid and destroy English villages who were not complying with the new regime. But even now the English resistance went on. In the fenlands, which were impassable marshes until they were drained centuries later, a group of Anglo-Saxon or Anglo-Danish outlaws had hidden away, led by a man called Hereward 'the Exile', or Hereward 'the Wake' as a later writer dubbed him. He had been a mercenary in Flanders. The stories go that when he returned he found his home had been destroyed and his family slaughtered by the Normans, so he went to an inn where they were carousing and killed some of them. With a band of guerrilla fighters a few hundred strong, he defied the Normans and outwitted their doomed attempts to capture or kill him. His daring and risky exploits brought him new followers and his base in the fens near Ely became a centre for raids on the Normans which cost them dearly. Eventually William had to come in person to supervise the siege and even enlisted the aid of a witch! Hereward repulsed the king on one occasion, but eventually he escaped with only a few of his men into a great forest called *Bruneswald* in the East Midlands. This all sounds very Robin Hood, but Hereward was not the only Anglo-Saxon resistance fighter. Edric the Wild or the Forester was still at large as well, out on the Welsh border. In fact, these great forests and fenlands were the only refuge now for English outlaws, those who continued to defy the Norman regime.

Edric's original name was Edric 'Guilda', which in Latin is *Sylvaticus* or 'the Forester'. Those English nobles who had not fled abroad, hoping for another English rebellion, hid out in the remote dense forests where they hunted, attacked 'French' convoys, robbed travellers and became the prototype for Robin Hood and his Merry Men (they perhaps worshipped some manifestation of the Virgin Mary). There were doubtless thousands of such men (and perhaps women) all over England, but as the Norman grip on England tightened they eventually dwindled and became part of the rich tapestry of folklore and legend. Hereward and Edric both seem to have surrendered. Hereward was murdered by a 'French' knight, but Edric's fate remains mysterious. Some say he never died, and still rides out when England goes to war, a ghost of a vanished civilisation.

99. The Normans Made Sure They Were Here to Stay

The Anglo-Saxons and their Anglo-Danish neighbours now had no choice but to submit to the reality of a brutal occupation by a hostile foreign power. The Vikings had at least been people you could talk to, but the Normans spoke French and refused to learn English, or at least the crucial political aristocracy around the king did. No more than a dozen men owned most of England and a group of just a few hundred powerful men dominated all national life. The loss of influence of English noblemen was striking, though William was not a complete tyrant – he even gave Edgar the Aetheling a pension! Vast areas of England were made over to afforestation so that the king could enjoy the Normans' favourite pastime – hunting! A chronicler wrote that William 'loved the high-deer as if he were their father'. A local militia of forest-keepers watched over the king's rights in the forests, and tracked outlaws and brigands, and their punishments were frightful. In ancient towns modern 'French-towns' were built beside the English areas so that the two populations did not have to mix; they even worshipped in different churches. There was also no chance of running into the 'French' in the alehouse. The Normans abhorred ale and only drank in *bouteilleries*, taverns that sold wine. In general, the lot of the common Englishman was probably harder at first, though the Normans did abolish slavery, so they weren't all bad!

100. The Anglo-Saxons Preserved Their Language and Culture

All of this probably sounds a bit sad after so many centuries of glorious history, but there were some things the Anglo-Saxons could keep, despite everything the Normans did to them. One crucial thing was their language. Although some French words entered the English language, on the whole the Anglo-Saxons refused to speak anything but English. In the twelfth century an English lay-preacher called Layamon decided to write a history of England and of Britain before it, a long poem called a *Brut*. He wrote it in English, the despised language of his own people, and later other Englishmen followed his example, among them Chaucer, Langland and Shakespeare. Thanks to them, the English language became one of the most widely spoken in the world, and its literature contains some of the jewels of the written word.

The Normans gradually made concessions. Edgar's sister, Margaret, married Malcolm III of Scotland and so the Anglo-Saxon royal line continued and their daughter, Matilda, was married to Henry I, William's fourth son. Because of this Queen Elizabeth II is a direct descendant of Alfred the Great, and possibly Cerdic! It is truly extraordinary that we still have this personal link to the Anglo-Saxons, but we have much more than that. Because the Anglo-Saxons and Vikings mainly built using timber, there is very little to show for over six centuries of history, except a few churches and large earthworks like Offa's Dyke and Wat's Dyke. But the names of nearly all of England's towns, villages and even fields have remained stubbornly Anglo-Saxon, and we still have Anglo-Saxon names for days of the week. A large proportion of the present-day population of the United Kingdom are still direct descendants of the Anglo-Saxons. In 1939 the excavations at Sutton Hoo in Suffolk brought vividly home to us just what a rich and splendid culture it was which gave birth to the first English kingdoms. More recently the Staffordshire Hoard, with its astonishing complexity and stunning beauty, has captured the imagination of the public, forcing us to re-evaluate a 'Dark Age' and 'barbarian' culture.

The Anglo-Saxons were not 'barbarians'. In brutal, bloody and prolonged conflicts with their British neighbours, between their seven kingdoms and then with the Vikings, they had learned resilience, patient endurance, unswerving loyalty to their kings and then their God. They gave birth to the first developed nation state in Europe, and by their industry and artisanship created a unique culture and civilisation, wealthy and sophisticated, renowned for its learning and works of art. It was this very success which rendered them vulnerable, and Ethelred's long and disastrous reign undermined the very institution which had enabled English dominance – its monarchy. Edward's failure to produce an heir doomed the Anglo-Saxons, but they adapted to Danish and then Norman rule, until the invaders were incorporated, until they too called themselves 'English'. Perhaps of all their achievements, their stubborn refusal to let go of their native language and culture was the most important of all.